From Shore to Shore

*Liturgies, Litanies and Prayers
from Around the World*

Compiled and edited by
Kate Wyles
USPG

Published in Great Britain in 2003
Society for Promoting Christian Knowledge
Holy Trinity Church
Marylebone Road
London NW1 4DU

USPG is a major mission agency of the Anglican Church
and works in more than 50 countries overseas

USPG, 157 Waterloo Road, London SE1 8XA
Registered charity number 234518

British Library Cataloguing-in-Publication Data

A catalogue record for this book is available from the British Library

ISBN 0–281–05393–6

1 3 5 7 9 10 8 6 4 2

Typeset by Wilmaset Ltd, Birkenhead, Wirral
Printed in Great Britain by
The Cromwell Press, Trowbridge, Wiltshire

Contents

Introduction

From Shore to Shore is a compilation of liturgies, litanies and prayers gathered from the church around the world.

You can use the material either for your own private prayer and reflection, or within church worship. Sometimes it will be appropriate to use the whole liturgy; at other times it may be better to use just part of it. *From Shore to Shore* includes orders of service for Holy Communion, and services that help people consider specific issues, such as HIV/AIDS and the environment. The selection of prayers and litanies are organized under liturgical headings to help busy worship leaders in their preparation. Above all we encourage you to be bold in the way you use the material in this book, adapting it to fit your local situation.

From Shore to Shore is an ecumenical resource that includes material used by Anglican, Catholic, Methodist and United Churches world-wide. Each of the respective liturgies usually comes from one culture, but sometimes the material is compiled from different parts of the world. All prayers and litanies contained in the book were contributed by Christians around the world, including missionaries, some of whom have served in Britain and Ireland.

From Shore to Shore was compiled by USPG, an Anglican mission agency, during its 300th anniversary year. It is offered as a thanksgiving for the great riches and insights of churches in other parts of the world. We hope that you will find this resource fresh and exciting, even unexpected in places and that it will give you a deeper enthusiasm for joining in with worship that echoes from shore to shore.

Kate Wyles
USPG

Orders of Service for Holy Communion

A LITURGY TO CELEBRATE LIBERATION, BARBADOS

When the British passed the Abolition of Slavery Act of 1834, it was felt that the former slaves would not know how to use their new-found freedom, so a six-year 'apprenticeship' was to follow before full freedom was conferred. This proved to be a grave error and saw the treatment of the former slaves deteriorate still further. This matter was brought to the British Parliament, and the Emancipation Act was passed on 1 August 1838, bringing the Apprenticeship to a premature end.

In recent years this date has gained more and more prominence in the Caribbean community and today 1 August is observed as a national holiday in most of the Caribbean. The Sunday closest to this date is often observed as Emancipation Sunday. It was for such a Sunday that the following liturgy was created.

The celebration of Emancipation Day is a fitting symbol of the first freed slaves who took to the streets on the morning of the end of Apprenticeship. The tone of the liturgy is one of rejoicing in the power of God's might. At the same time it is a reminder of the level that people can stoop to in an effort to gain economic well-being.

The triumph of the human spirit in the Caribbean through the experience of slavery demonstrates the resilience of a people devastated year after year by hurricanes yet always rejoicing, for to the people of the Caribbean life is to be lived. Through this liturgy congregations may remember our calling to full humanity and in so doing give to each human person the dignity and love that is bound up in being human.

CALL TO WORSHIP

For freedom Christ has set us free.
Stand firm, therefore, and do not submit again to a yoke of slavery.

Blessed be God: Father, Son and Holy Spirit.
Alleluia! Alleluia!

**And blessed be his Kingdom, now and for ever. Amen.
Alleluia! Alleluia!**

COLLECT

Almighty and most loving God,
through your Son Jesus, who came among us as a slave,
choosing rather to serve his disciples than to be served by them;
help us in our weakness not to seek to oppress others,
nor to make peace with any form of exploitation,
but in all things earnestly and of our own free will,
to seek to serve each other following Christ's good example;
this we ask in the name of Jesus Christ our Lord.
Amen.

CONFESSION

O God of our forebears, who in every generation sets us free to
    live the life for which we are created,
we confess that we have not accepted that freedom as we ought.
We have not accepted it for ourselves, neither have we set others
    free.
We have enslaved our sisters and brothers through our thoughts,
    our words and our actions.
We are very sorry for our misuse of your gracious gift,
and we ask your forgiveness and your help to live in true
    freedom.
For it is only when we are truly free in ourselves
that others are set free.

ABSOLUTION

May the God who led the slaves out of slavery into new life
lead you through his forgiving love out of your bondage,
that you may experience the joy of the eternal life
that he has given you in Christ Jesus our liberator.
Amen.

GREAT THANKSGIVING (Eucharistic Prayer)

The Lord be with you.
And also with you.
Lift up your hearts.
We lift them up to the Lord.

Let us give thanks to the Lord our God.
It is right to give him thanks and praise.

It is right, and a good and joyful thing, always and everywhere to
give you thanks, almighty and everlasting God:
Therefore we praise you, joining our voices with angels
and archangels and with all the company of heaven,
who forever sing this hymn to proclaim the glory of your name:

Holy, holy, holy Lord, God of power and might;
heaven and earth are full of your glory.
Hosanna in the highest.
Blessed is he who comes in the name of the Lord.
Hosanna in the highest.

Creator God, God of our mothers and fathers,
through the ages you have called our ancestors
to be faithful to your will, that you may bless them.
You called Abraham
and brought him from his father's house to a land
you had chosen, where you blessed him.
You brought hope to Sarah in her old age,
declaring once more your wondrous love
for your people in the common things of life.
When Joseph was enslaved, you were with him,
and at the appointed time you led him out of bondage
to be the prince of Egypt.
You later raised up your servant Moses,
whom you had chosen to lead your people
out of bondage in Egypt,
to receive your commandments
and declare them to your people.
From this people, you forged a mighty nation
to declare your will to the world.
Throughout the ages you continued to raise women and men
to lead your people out of various forms of bondage.
Yet we failed to be faithful to you.
We turned away from your will and neglected to follow
the path you had chosen for us.

Your Son Jesus, the Christ, came among us as flesh and blood,
showing us an example of perfect obedience,
and declaring that we were born free,

not to be enslaved by sin, but to bind ourselves to the love of God.
Through him you freed us from the power of sin;
even death itself was to be no eternal shackle for your people.
He conquered death and the grave.
In him, you have brought us out of error into truth,
out of sin into righteousness,
out of death into life.
His triumph makes us worthy to stand in your presence to give
　　you thanks.
Therefore we ask you to hear us,
and sanctify with your Holy Spirit this bread and this cup.

For on the night he was betrayed he took bread,
blessed it and gave it to his disciples,
saying, 'Take, eat: this is my body which is given for you.
Do this for the remembrance of me.'

Then he took the cup of wine, and when he had blessed it, said,
'This is my blood of the new covenant, which is shed for you
and for many for the forgiveness of sins.
Do this, whenever you drink it, for the remembrance of me.'

Therefore, loving Creator, according to his command,

we remember *his* death,
we proclaim *his* resurrection,
we await *his* coming in glory,

and we ask you to look with favour on this sacrifice of praise and
thanksgiving which we bring before you.
Bless us who will share in this sacred meal,
and grant us so to be filled with your Spirit,
that our lives may be living examples of your presence in this
　　world.
Bless and inspire us, that we may proclaim your reign in this world,
making no compromise with injustice.
Bless the church which you have left and fill it with the spirit of
　　unity,
that those things which demonstrate the diversity of our human
　　race may not be used as points which divide us,
but as pillars of our unity in Christ.

We thank you for all persons who in every age
received your word and committed themselves

to the deliverance of others from bondage.
We remember those who gave their lives
for the removal of slavery from our land.

Pour out your Spirit upon the whole earth
and make it your new creation.
That with all your people
of every race, class, language and nation,
we may share the banquet you have promised;
through Christ, with Christ, and in Christ,
and join together in songs of everlasting praise.

**Blessing and honour and glory and power
be yours for ever and ever.
Amen.**

FINAL BLESSING

May the God who has set you free from the yoke of slavery
walk with you into the realm of his glory,
that you may witness the joy of the free life in God
for which you have been created.
The blessing of God the creator, liberator and
sustainer be with you now and throughout eternity.
Amen.

A LITURGY FROM THE INDEPENDENT
CHURCH OF THE PHILIPPINES

PREPARATION

Blessed be God: Father, Son and Holy Spirit.
And blessed be his Kingdom, now and for ever. Amen.

CONFESSION

**Almighty God,
to you all hearts are open,
all desires known,
and from you no secrets are hid.
Cleanse our hearts by your Holy Spirit,**

that we may truly love you,
and worthily praise your holy name
through Christ our Lord,
Amen.

Hear what our Lord Jesus Christ says:
'You shall love the Lord your God with all your heart
and with all your mind and with all your strength.'
This is the first and great commandment.
And the second is like it:
'You shall love your neighbour as yourself.'
On these two commandments depend all the Law and the
    Prophets.
Let us humbly confess our sins against God and our neighbours.

Silence is kept for a time

We confess to God Almighty,
to all the saints,
and to each other,
that we have sinned
in what we have thought,
in what we have said,
in what we have done,
and in what we have failed to do;
and it was our own fault.
Therefore we beg God to have mercy on us,
and we ask all the saints
to pray for us to the Lord our God. Amen.

Almighty God have mercy on you,
forgive you your sins,
and keep you in eternal life;
through Jesus Christ our Lord.
Amen.

GLORIA IN EXCELSIS

THE LITURGY OF THE WORD OF GOD
The Lord be with you.
And also with you.
Let us pray.

Lord God, as you anointed kings and called prophets of old,
lead us to recognize our true representatives and authentic
    leaders;
men and women who love your people and can walk with them,
who feel their pain and share their joys,
who dream their dreams and strive to accompany them to their
    common goal.
In your fire – with your spirit, embolden and commission us to
    transform our political system,
to serve your people
and to bring real glory to your name.
Amen.

READING

CREED

INTERCESSIONS

HOLY EUCHARIST

PEACE

All stand
Brothers and sisters, we are the Body of Christ; by one Spirit we
    were all baptized into one Body.
Let us keep the unity of the Spirit in the bond of peace.
The peace of the Lord be always with you.
And also with you.

OFFERTORY

Let us with gladness present the offerings of our life and work to
the Lord.

At the offering of the bread

Eternal God,
you caused the grain to grow,
and from it we have made this bread:
We offer it to you
that it may become for us the Bread of Life.
Grant that we who shall receive it
may be united in the bond of love. Amen.

At the offering of the wine

God Almighty,
accept this wine we have made from your gifts:
may it become our spiritual drink,
that we who shall receive it
may be refreshed and renewed for your service. Amen.

Pray that our sacrifice may be acceptable to God the Father
  Almighty.
May the Lord receive our sacrifice
for the praise and glory of his name,
for our good, and that of all his Church.

GREAT THANKSGIVING

The merciful goodness of the Lord endures
for ever and ever on those who fear him,
and his righteousness from generation to generation.
Even on those who keep his covenant,
and remember his commandments and do them.

The Lord has set his throne in heaven; and his kingship has
  dominion over all.
Praise the Lord, you angels of his: you mighty ones who do his
  bidding, and listen to the voice of his word.

Praise the Lord, all you his hosts, you ministers of his who do his
  will.
Praise the Lord, all you works of his, in all places of his
  dominion,
Praise the Lord!

The Lord be with you.
And also with you.

Lift up your hearts.
We lift them up to the Lord.

Let us give thanks to the Lord our God.
It is right to give him thanks and praise.

It is truly right, it is our duty and our joy ...

Proper preface as appointed.

(*Martyrs:* And now we give you thanks that in the witness of your
martyrs who followed Christ even to death you revealed your
power made perfect in our human weakness.)

Therefore, with angels and archangels and with all the company
of heaven, we joyfully proclaim your glory, evermore praising
you and saying:

Holy, holy, holy Lord,
God of power and might;
heaven and earth are full of your glory.
Hosanna in the highest.
Blessed is he who comes in the name of the Lord.
Hosanna in the highest.

All glory is yours, almighty God, heavenly Father,
for of your love and mercy
you gave your only Son Jesus Christ
to take our nature upon him,
and to suffer death upon the Cross
for our redemption.
He made there, by the one offering of himself,
a full and perfect sacrifice for the whole world;
and he instituted and commanded us to continue
a memorial of his precious death and sacrifice,
until his coming again.

For in the night in which he was betrayed,
he took bread;
and when he had given thanks to you,
he broke it, and gave it to his disciples and said:
'Take, eat, this is my Body which is given for you. Do this to
    remember me.'
After supper he took the cup;
and when he had given thanks, he gave it to them and said:
'Drink this, all of you; for this is my Blood of the new covenant
which is poured out for you and for many
for the forgiveness of sins.
Whenever you drink it, do this to remember me.'

Christ has died, Christ is risen, Christ will come.

Therefore, Lord and heavenly Father,
we your humble servants
celebrate the memorial your Son commanded;
having in remembrance his blessed passion
and precious death,
his mighty resurrection and glorious ascension,
and looking for his coming in glory,
we offer you this Bread of Life
and this Cup of Salvation.
And with these gifts we offer ourselves,
asking you to accept upon your heavenly altar,
this our sacrifice of praise and thanksgiving.
Gracious Father, by the power of your Holy Spirit,
bless and sanctify this bread and wine,
that they may be to us the most precious Body and Blood of your
    Son Jesus Christ.
May all who receive this Holy Communion
be filled with your grace and heavenly blessing
and be made one body with him,
that he may dwell in us and we in him.

And although we are not worthy
to offer you any sacrifice,
yet we ask you to accept this our duty and service.
Through Jesus Christ our Lord;
by him and with him,
and in him,
in the unity of the Holy Spirit.
All honour and glory is yours, O Father Almighty, now and for
    ever.
(*Loudly*) **Amen.**

The people may kneel.
Silence.

THE LORD'S PRAYER

BREAKING OF THE BREAD
Lord, we ask you to deliver us from all evil
and to grant peace in our time.
By the help of your mercy
keep us free from sin and safe from anxiety;

Through your Son Jesus Christ our Lord,
who lives and reigns with you and the Holy Spirit,
one God, now and for ever.
Amen.

Lamb of God, you take away the sin of the world;
have mercy on us.
Lamb of God, you take away the sin of the world;
have mercy on us.
Lamb of God, you take away the sin of the world;
Grant us your peace.

Silence

The gifts of God for the people of God.
Take them in remembrance that Christ gives himself for you,
and feed on him in your hearts by faith,
with thanksgiving.

DISMISSAL

The Lord be with you.
And also with you.

Let us pray.
Eternal God our Father,
you have accepted us as living members
of the Body of your Son Jesus Christ our Lord,
and you have nourished us with the Sacrament
of his victorious life.
May we now be bread broken and given to the world,
may your love in us heal the wounds we have made,
may your words on our lips speak peace to all.
Send us with vision and strength to serve your
Son in the least of his brothers and sisters.
So will your name be praised and glorified,
now and in time to come, until all be fulfilled in your Kingdom.
Amen.

Blessed be the name of the Lord
Now and forever.

Our help is in the Name of the Lord
Who made heaven and earth.

The peace of God which surpasses all understanding
keep you strong in the knowledge and love of God,
and his Son Jesus Christ our Lord.
And the blessing of God Almighty,
the Father, the Son and the Holy Spirit,
be upon you and remain with you always.
Amen.

The Lord be with you.
And also with you.

Go now to love and serve the Lord.
Thanks be to God.

⌇

THE SRI LANKAN WORKERS' MASS

The Workers' Mass comes from of the Christian Workers'
Fellowship (CWF) of Sri Lanka. The CWF was formed in 1958
through a group of predominantly English-speaking Christian
workers in central Colombo. One of its first acts was to publish a
pamphlet called *The Christian Worker and the Trade Union*. A
journal, *Christian Worker* was also started. From the beginning, the
movement was outside church structures but rooted in the biblical
themes of social justice and equality. It established close contact
with trade unions, working class political parties and organiza-
tions concerned with social action.

The Workers' Mass was created in this early period as a May
Day celebration. It has been held in Colombo on 1 May every year
since 1960. In 1971 and 1990, it was the only public celebration
held, as all other May Day meetings had been banned because of
political crisis. Most significant is that clergy sympathetic to the
aims of the CWF from all the churches in Sri Lanka concelebrate
the Mass. It is also usual for Buddhists and Hindus to be present,
embraced by the inclusivity of the liturgy.

Today, *Christian Worker* continues to be produced. The CWF has
centres in various parts of the country. These bring together
people from Sri Lanka's four religions and seek to promote
community, human development and social justice.

This translation of the Eucharistic Prayer attempts to bring out
something of its spirit from the original Sinhala.

Glossary

Dharma   'Truth' is the nearest equivalent for its usage here.

Rishis   Another word for sage, revered teacher.

Sat-chit-ananda   Literally 'being – consciousness – bliss'; a three-fold characterization of God in Hinduism.

Tanha   Literally 'craving, selfish clinging' – the root of human dis-ease according to Buddhism.

Taraka   The one who not only crosses over to the further shore, from suffering to speaking once more to his comrades of freedom, but also makes others cross over as liberator or saviour.

THE GREAT THANKSGIVING (Eucharistic Prayer)

Let us all now lift our hearts.
To our God we lift our hearts.

Cleansing fire of the universe,
Preserver and life-giver
O Holy God, we worship you,
Offering heartfelt praise and thanks.
Of all reality the heart
O Dharma eternal and true
Sat-chit-ananda are you.

O most gracious God, truth primeval,
Springhead of all life,
Nourishing us, our Mother,
Of all beings Father.

From darkness drear you bring forth light.
From chaos you draw out order.
Out of Nature's beauty speaking
into fellowship us calling.

Your creation to guide and lead,
Your blessed humanity's seed,
Gifting memory, reason, feeling,
Skill for us as partners seating.

Lured by Tanha from our calling,
Blinded, led astray to failing,
Dharma's light our path then guiding,
From bondage to freedom leading.

Spoke through Buddhas, sages of old, Rishis,
Prophets who God's will showed,
Freedom struggles history disclosed
Revolutions moving our world.

Poor and like us born of woman,
Knowing toil, a worker by profession,
Dharma, Truth and Way became human,
Named Jesus and Taraka by acclaim.

For us to truly touch and see,
Food and guests at our meal was he.
Among us a living memory,
In peace as comrades how to live
The human model he did give.
He came the news of God's reign to proclaim,
Began the new age that we had to gain,
For this he suffered death and pain,
To liberate us Jesus came.

To our world, this manifest Dharma,
Jesus by name, our own brother,
The night he was betrayed,
The night of his arrest,
The night he faced death,
Taking bread and thanks rendering,
Breaking the bread for its sharing,
Spoke these words when he was giving:
'Take, eat comrades,' this bread breaking.
'It is my body for you.'
Taking up the cup he then said:
'This cup is a pledge of the age new,
This is my blood poured out for you,
Drink of it all of you,
Remember me whenever you this do.'
His death and victory re-enacting
His coming in judgement anticipating,
Bread and cup as he bid us here, proffering,
We pledge to birth the new age in this offering.

Accept, O God, this sacrifice of
Thanksgiving and praise.
Quicken and awaken with your Spirit's power

This people, bread and cup,
That they truly all become,
In flesh and in blood, the very Dharma
Transformed by your mighty power.
Awakened are we.
Arisen are we.
The Dharma and we are now one!

United now with the oppressed ones,
And in their struggle to birth the new age,
We declare freedom for all and a common weal
In partaking now of this freedom meal!
With the most blessed Mother who of freedom sang,
Whose brave hymn of praise and liberty rang
With the liberated ones who illumined our world,
Now with all who ever were,
Who are with us and will be
With the whole creation,
Joyously we dance and sing:

Holy, Holy, Holy God,
Great God of might and power,
All space and all time
Show forth your glory.
Amen.

⟻

A CELTIC LITURGY IN THE TRADITION
OF THE CARMINA GADELICA

The ancient Christian Celts talked about the 'deep wisdom of
God' as being the *Imago Dei* (the Image of God) that lives actively
in the soul of every individual and the whole of Creation. The
body of their worship – the prayers, ceremonies and rituals – was
called *mysterion*, reflecting the Greek origins of the original
introduction of Christianity to the six Celtic countries of Ireland,
Wales, Scotland, Isle of Man, Cornwall and Brittany. It is only
later, in the seventh century, with the triumph of the Latin Church
in the kingdoms of Britain, that these began to be repressed and

replaced by the Mediterranean forms which were called sacraments and daily offices.

For the Celts, life was worship and worship was to be immersed in the *mysterion*, because God desires to speak daily to all humans from the place of deep wisdom. Even the minutest activities of the morning like kindling the fire for a new day or sweeping the steps were the means of participating in the *mysterion*, the deep wisdom of God.

This order of service is an example of Celtic imagination, both old and new. It draws from ancient texts. Its contemporary existence also is true to the Celtic spirit of being open to new impulses and new arrangements. This liturgy provides a form of how, in the words of the Collect for the Church, we might 'see and know that things which were cast down are being raised up, and things which had grown old are being made new'. Therefore, this liturgy is meant to be a starting point, and not an ending; an invitation to adapt and above all to imagine how a worshipping community might come alive with the richness of images and invitations from the Celtic tradition.

LITURGY OF THE WORD

GATHERING

Blessed be God,
The One who creates us,
The Spirit who is poured into our hearts,
The Son who is born in us.
Glory to God for ever and ever.

PREPARATION

Rune before Prayer:
    I am bending the knee.
    In the eye of the Father who created me
    I am bending the knee.
    In the eye of the Spirit who enlivened me
    I am bending the knee.
    In the eye of the Son who redeemed me
    In friendship and affection.
    Through our own anointed one with us, O God.
    Bestow upon us fullness in our need,

Love towards God,
The affection of God,
The smile of God,
The wisdom of God,
The grace of God,
The will of God,
To do in the world
As angels and saints do in heaven;
Each shade and light,
Each day and night,
Each time and kindness,
Give us your Spirit.

An anthem may be sung here

The Collect for the Day may be used

God be with us. Amen.
The Lord be with you.
And with your spirit too.

Bless, O Chief of generous chiefs,
Ourselves and everything a-near us,
Bless us in all our actions,
Make Thou us safe for ever,
Make Thou us safe for ever
from every brownie and banshee,
from every evil wish and sorrow,
from every nymph and water-wraith,
from every fairy-mouse and grass-mouse,
from every fairy-mouse and grass-mouse.
From every troll among the hills,
from every siren hard pressing us,
from every ghoul within the glens,
O! save us till the end of our days,
O! save us till the end of our days.
Amen.

READING

From Scripture or from the Celtic tradition

HOMILY

AFFIRMATION OF FAITH

I believe O God of all gods that you are:
The eternal creator of life.
I believe O God of all gods that you are:
The eternal source of love.
I believe O God of all gods that you are:
The eternal reconciler of peace.
I believe O God of all gods that you are:
The eternal fountain of joy.
I believe O God of all gods that you are:
The eternal companion of the saints.
I believe O God of all gods that you are:
The eternal God strong to save.
I believe O God of all gods that you are:
The eternal God of my life.

CONFESSION OF SIN

Let us confess our sins against God, ourselves and our neighbour.
God of all mercy,
We confess that we have sinned against you,
resisting your will with our lives.
We have not honoured you in ourselves, in each other,
and in the world you have made.
Reach out your saving arm
and rescue us from our sins.
Forgive, restore and strengthen us
through our saviour Jesus Christ
that we may abide in your love and serve only your will
for your people and creation.
Amen.

ABSOLUTION

May your heart stir quietly now having thought upon the things
    you have done and left undone.
May God remove from you the things that troubled your soul,
    that in penitence you might be restored to life to serve him and
    know his love.
So may God forgive you your sins and release you to delight in his
    world.
Amen.

PEACE

Peace be upon all within this house,
Peace to keep you safe from harm,
Peace upon your neighbours, all,
Peace to the world in which we live.
The peace of the High Chief of Heaven be with you.
And also with you.

OFFERTORY

To whom shall we offer oblations in the name of Michael on high?
We will give tithe of our means to the forsaken illustrious one.
We will give this bread and this wine, for they are ourselves, our
    being, our all.
Because of all that we have seen of his peace and of his mercy,
Lift thou our souls to thee, O High Chief of Heaven.

Never leave us.
Remember us in the mountain;
Under thy wing shield us;
Rock of Truth, do not forsake us;
Our wish it is to be ever near Thee.

GREAT THANKSGIVING

May the High King of Heaven be with you.
And also with you.
Lift up your hearts.
We lift them to our God.
Let us adore and exalt our God.
It is right to give our thanks and praise.

Now we must praise you, the warden of heaven's realm.
The Creator's might and your mind's thought;
the glorious works of your hands, the Spirit and the Son;
how of every wonder you, the creator, the eternal, laid the
    foundations,
shaped the earth, for the children of earth,
heaven as our roof,
the middle-world our home.
We place all of heaven and earth within your power:
the sun with its brightness,
the snow with its whiteness,

the fire with all the strength it has,
the lightning with its rapid wrath,
the winds with their swiftness along their path,
the sea with it deepness,
the earth with its starkness.
All these we place before you,
and with all the hosts of heaven do we sing:

Holy, Holy, Holy One,
God of power and might;
heaven and earth are full of your glory.
Hosanna in the highest.
Blessed is the One who comes in the name of God.
Hosanna in the highest.

Glory and thanksgiving be to you, most loving Father,
for the gift of your Son born in human flesh of our sister, Mary.
He is the Word existing beyond time, both source and final
purpose, bringing to wholeness all that is made.
Obedient to your will he died upon the Cross.
By your power you raised him from the dead.
He broke the bonds of evil and set your people free
to be his Body in the world.
On the night when he was given up to death,
knowing that his hour had come, having loved his own,
he loved them to the end.
At supper with his disciples he took bread and offered you thanks.
He broke the bread and gave it to them, saying:
'Take, eat. This is my Body: it is broken for you.'
After supper, he took the cup, he offered you thanks,
and gave it to them saying:
'Drink this, all of you. This is my Blood of the new covenant;
it is poured out for you, and for all,
that sins may be forgiven.
Do this in remembrance of me.'
We now obey your Son's command.
We recall his blessed passion and death,
his glorious resurrection and ascension;
and we look for the coming of his Kingdom.
Made one with him, we offer you these gifts,
and with them ourselves, a single, holy,
and living sacrifice.

Hear us, most merciful father, and send your Holy Spirit upon us and upon this bread and this wine, that, overshadowed by its life-giving power, they may be the Body and Blood of your Son, and we may be kindled with the fire of your love and renewed for the service of your Kingdom.
Help us, who are baptized into the fellowship of Christ's Body, live and work to your praise and glory;
May we grow together in unity and love until at last, in your new creation, we enter into your heritage in the company of the Virgin Mary, the apostles and prophets,
(*saints' names may be added here*)
and all our brothers and sisters living and departed.

Through Jesus Christ our Lord, with whom, and in whom, in the unity of the Holy Spirit, all honour and glory be to you, Lord of all ages, world without end.
Amen.

THE LORD'S PRAYER

THE BREAKING OF THE BREAD

The living bread is broken for the life of the world.
Lord, unite us in this sign.

COMMUNION

POST-COMMUNION PRAYER

May the strength of God pilot us,
may the power of God preserve us,
may the wisdom of God instruct us,
may the hand of God protect us,
may the way of God direct us,
may the host of God guard us against the snares of the evil one
and the temptations of the world.
This day and for evermore.
Amen.

BLESSING

The Father on you his blessing bestow,
the Spirit's presence to you show,
the Son his love towards you flow.

On you, and all the folk you know,
on you, and all who around you go,
the blessing may you know.

DISMISSAL

The King of Heaven goes before us and waits for us.
Come, follow me into the world to continue our service with all of
   Creation.
Thanks be to God.

Other Orders of Service

TOGETHER WE ARE STRONG
An Australian Liturgy for International Women's Day

International Women's Day, held each year on 8 March, provides a focused opportunity to celebrate the achievements of women, to consider the contemporary social and economic concerns of women and to seek for justice for women all over the world.

The following liturgy, produced by the Uniting Church of Australia, is based on Psalm 27 and Luke 13.31–35. The liturgy can be used as a short reflection, or as part of an expanded liturgy for a Sunday worship service.

Seven candles are required. The central candle is white, while the six candles around it are alternately purple and green. In a liturgical context, purple is the colour of Lent and white the colour of the Christ candle. Purple and green were the colours worn by the suffragettes in the UK who struggled for women's right to vote during the late nineteenth and early twentieth centuries. In the context of International Women's Day, purple stands for justice and dignity and green stands for hope. The colour white is also sometimes used as a symbol of commitment.

GATHERING TOGETHER

The candles are placed on a central table. Before the liturgy begins, the central candle is lit.

We come before you, God of ancient times, acknowledging your presence with us.
We come before you, God of the present, believing in your presence with us.
We come before you, God of the future, hoping for your presence with us.

Celebrating
Living
Journeying
We are women/people on the way.

Fighting
Caring
Challenging
We are women/people on the way.

Hurting
Believing
Exploring
We are women/people on the way.

Sharing
Understanding
Nurturing
We are women/people on the way.

A song may be sung here

WELCOME AND INTRODUCTION

LITANY OF REMEMBERING
We wait
To see justice prevail.

We are strong together
As we challenge oppression.

Our hearts take courage
For the work still to do.

We remember today:

Women who are victims of domestic violence; women who are victims of psychological, physical and sexual abuse – women struggling to live in their violated bodies, to forget the words, the frightened looks of their children, the unwelcome touching...
We wait...
Together we are strong, and our hearts take courage.

A candle is lit and a time of silence follows

Women who have no access to education, and are therefore economically disadvantaged – women seeking to make a better life for themselves, for their family, facing the hopelessness of unfulfilled dreams and aspirations...

We wait...
Together we are strong, and our hearts take courage.

A candle is lit and a time of silence follows

Women who are bound by oppressive laws; and women who are not free to participate in decisions that affect their lives – women vulnerable to those in power, who long to speak but are silenced...
We wait...
Together we are strong, and our hearts take courage.

A candle is lit and a time of silence follows

Women who have fought the unjust structures of society and government to bring changes to the disadvantaged – women willing to advocate for change, who sign petitions, who speak up again, and again and again...
We rise up...
Together we are strong, and our hearts take courage.

A candle is lit and a time of silence follows

Women who resist the pressures to conform to others' expectations; women who have learned of the power there is in self-assertion and self-discovery, who insist on the rightness of possessing themselves...
We rise up...
Together we are strong, and our hearts take courage.

A candle is lit and a time of silence follows

Women who see the possibilities, and invite us to join them – women weaving a symbol of hope ... singing, dancing, celebrating...
We rise up...
Together we are strong, and our hearts take courage.

A candle is lit and a time of silence follows

We work and we wait, to see justice prevail.
We work and we wait, for we are strong together as we challenge
   oppression.
We work and we wait, and our hearts take courage for the work
   still to do.

God of grace and peace,
hear our rememberings
and our calling out for justice.
Enliven our world
with your creative spirit.
That all people will remember
that we are made in your image,
and we are worthy of honour and acceptance.
In the name of Christ.
Amen.

A song may be sung here

THE BLESSING

Gather us to you as a mother hen,
under your sheltering wings,
and shield us as we go,
for we are women/people on the way.

We go from here,
blessed for the journey
that lies before us, and
strengthened for the challenges
we may yet face.

We go with
the love of the God who nurtures us,
the presence of the God who protects us,
the sustenance of the God who inspires us.
Amen.

A CARIBBEAN ORDER OF MORNING WORSHIP, JAMAICA

Worship songs from the Caribbean could be used with this service. *Caribbean Praise* is a good resource for this. See 'Vengan, vengan todos' (Come now everybody), by Lois Kroehler, Cuba, No. 99 in *Caribbean Praise*.

Worshippers sit in silence or with background music being played. A group member brings the first symbol, the Bible, and places it on the table or altar.

CALL TO WORSHIP

For as the rain and the snow come down from heaven,
And do not return there until they have watered the earth,
Making it bring forth and sprout,
Giving seed to the sower and bread to the eater;
So shall my word be that goes out from my mouth.
It shall not return to me empty,
But it shall accomplish that which I purpose,
And succeed in the thing for which I sent it.

Isaiah 55.10–11

Silence

The second symbol, a lighted candle, is placed on the table or altar

You are the light of the world. A city built on a hill cannot be hid.
No one after lighting a lamp puts it under the bushel basket, but
    on the lampstand, and it gives light to all in the house.
In the same way, let your light shine before others, so that they
    may see your good works and give glory to your Father in
    heaven.

Silence

The third symbol, a small cross, is placed on the table or altar

Christ Jesus humbled himself and became obedient to the point of
    death – even death on a cross.
Therefore God also highly exalted him and gave him the name
that is above every name, so that at the name of Jesus, every
knee should bend, in heaven and on earth and under the earth,
and every tongue should confess that Jesus Christ is Lord, to
the glory of God the Father.

Background music may be played

PRAYER

God of us all, we greet you every morning as the sun rises.
We experience your warmth, we glory in your light.
Around us in this island are beautiful hills, valleys, beaches,
    rivers, waterfalls, trees, flowers and fruits – symbols of your
    love and care.
Varied as they are, they also remind us that we do not have a
    monopoly on you. For other peoples around the world, you are
    God.
They, like us, sometimes experience your wrath, as in the violence
    of thunder storms, hurricanes, earthquakes and volcanoes. You
    are also a God of justice.
But even then your love breaks forth in our united efforts to
    rebuild our lives after a disaster. In mending broken lives, we
    draw closer to your Son, Jesus Christ.
His body was broken for us as an expression of your love in a
    most unusual way.

At the start of this day, grant us pardon for our sins.
Assure us again of your love, your mercy and your forgiveness:
We gratefully accept your gracious words of assurance,
'My son, my daughter, your sins are forgiven.
Go in peace, sin no more. Be healed.'
Thanks be to God. Amen.

Scripture reading

Song

PRAYERS OF INTERCESSION

*Led by a group member or shared by several. An appropriate response
after each prayer would be:*

In Christ's name, we pray. Amen.

After the final prayer:

God of us all,
You have heard our prayers for the people of the world.
Make us committed to continue our partnership with you,
so that together we might succeed in creating a new heaven and
    a new earth that will resound to your honour and glory.
Amen.

THE LORD'S PRAYER

Song

BLESSING

May the blessing of the One who created
the blue seas that wash our shores,
and the colourful mountain scenery
that adorns our landscape;
Be with us now and always.

May the blessing of the Son, who in his life shared
the joys and the sufferings that our
people experience daily;
Be with us now and always.

And may the blessing of the Spirit, who blows both
gently and fiercely through our atmosphere
to calm and to heal;
Be with us now and always, for ever.
Amen.

⤛

A SOUTH AFRICAN SERVICE
FOR WORLD AIDS DAY

AIDS, it is often said, is the modern leprosy. People suffering
from HIV/AIDS today experience many of the same reactions
as sufferers of leprosy did in the time of Jesus. Fear of
contagion leads to people with HIV/AIDS being shunned and
excluded by their societies. Like leprosy, it is a disease that
destroys relationships, families and societies as well as human
bodies.

This service, using prayers that are mainly from South Africa,
can be used on World AIDS Day, 1 December. It includes a quiz
(see Appendix) to help raise awareness about HIV/AIDS and
challenge prejudice caused by lack of understanding. Appropriate
readings are Mark 1.40–45 (see poem below), Isaiah 61.1–3,
Romans 8.31–39, Luke 10.30–37. Further prayers can be found in

the selection of Prayers and Litanies (see No. 19 on p. 89, No. 20 on p. 90, and No. 13 on p. 99), and could be used in place of those suggested for intercession, or in addition.

A large red candle should be decorated with a red ribbon before the service, and smaller candles may be available for members of the congregation to light during the intercessions. If you are using the quiz, paper and pens will need to be handed out as people arrive.

OPENING PRAYER

God of mercy and creator of all,
We gather here today to pray for all of us who are affected by
    HIV/AIDS:
For our loved ones;
for those who have died;
and for those of us who mourn;
for all of us who are caregivers;
for those of us who seek a cure: researchers, scientists and
    technicians;
for those of us who are fearful and prejudiced,
that being healed from fear, we may be empowered to support
    and care for each other.
We are here together in the name of Jesus Christ,
healer, teacher and way of salvation.
We are all sisters and brothers to him,
sons and daughters of the Living God.
Amen.

CONFESSION AND ABSOLUTION

We are called to bear witness to the Good News that no one is a
    stranger or an outsider,
and that in Jesus Christ all division and separation have been
    broken down.
In the face of the worldwide crisis of AIDS, we are called to be one
    people,
a whole people, none of whom is worthless.
Yet hardness of heart, discrimination and oppression prevent us
    from being who God calls us to be.
As we prepare to confess our sins, we come to God in prayer.

Lord of Compassion, we often represent you as a God of wrath.
Yet, you are the God of love, raising us to life;
and so we ask:
Lord, have mercy.
Lord have mercy.

Lord Jesus, you banish the fear that has often paralysed us.
In responding to the needs of all of us who are affected by HIV
    and AIDS,
when we falter, encourage us and strengthen us;
and so we ask:
Christ, have mercy.
Christ have mercy.

Spirit of unity, you build us up when we break down;
you unite when we divide; you comfort when we condemn;
and so we ask:
Lord, have mercy.
Lord have mercy.

Jesus said, 'You shall love the Lord your God with all your
heart, and with all your soul, and with all your mind.' This is
the first and great commandment. The second is like it, 'You
shall love your neighbour as yourself.' On these two
commandments depend the law and the prophets.

Let us call to mind and confess our sins, and firmly resolve to
keep God's commandments and live in love and peace with our
neighbour.

Silence

Almighty God, who forgives all who truly repent, have mercy on
    us.
Pardon our sins and set us free from them; confirm and
    strengthen us in all goodness and keep us in eternal life;
through Christ our Saviour, Amen.

READING

Based on Mark 1.40–41

'Lord, if you want to, you can make me clean.'

What made me say it to him I can't say –
I had not planned it – but the careful screen
I'd raised about my illness fell away.

I did not try to hide my rotting skin,
And saw my pain reflected in his face.
His eyes held mine (most others thought it sin
To look on filth like me) without a trace of fear.

Those eyes uncovered all I'd known
Of men's rejection, all that I could tell
Of misery so deep when hope had flown
And I had found myself alone in Hell.

'I want you to be clean'; his quiet word
was murmured soft – yet I knew God had heard.

John Tyler

QUIZ

INTERCESSIONS

We give thanks for the gospel of healing and liberation that is
    preached to the whole Church in the ministry of those with HIV
    and AIDS.
May we recognize that it is the body of Christ, that suffers at this
    time through HIV and AIDS.
It is the image of God in Christ, that is blasphemed in prejudice,
    oppression and poverty.
May we see in this crisis, loving God, not punishment but the
    place where God is most powerfully at work in Jesus Christ,
and where, as sisters and brothers, we can lead each other
to life in all its fullness, given in the same Christ our Lord.
Amen.

*Worshippers are invited to come forward in the silence after each prayer
to offer their own prayers and to light a candle.*

We pray for all who have lost loved ones to HIV/AIDS and for all
    who are now afraid to risk loving.
We remember those who have died from AIDS. We give thanks
    for the gift of their lives.

Silence

Lord, hear our prayer.

We pray for nurses and doctors, social workers and caregivers,
    and all those in the health-care professions who put their
    patients' needs ahead of their own.

Silence

Lord, hear our prayer.

We pray for those involved in medical research, as they struggle
to find a cure for HIV/AIDS.

Silence

Lord, hear our prayer.

We pray for those in Government, that they may respond with
compassion.

Silence

**Lord, accept these prayers for the sake of your Son,
Our Saviour, Jesus Christ. Amen.**

Loving God,
You show yourself in those who are vulnerable,
and make your home with the poor and weak of this world;
Warm our hearts with the fire of your spirit,
and help us to accept the challenges of AIDS.

Protect the healthy, calm the frightened,
give courage to those in pain, comfort the dying,
console the bereaved,
strengthen those who care for the sick.

May we, your people, using all our energy and imagination,
and trusting in your steadfast love,
be united with one another in conquering all disease and fear.

We make this prayer in the name of one who has borne all our
wounds,
and whose Spirit strengthens and guides us,
now and for ever.
Amen.

CLOSING PRAYER

May the love and compassion of God be ours,
may the strength and healing of the Spirit be ours,
may the life-giving words of the Son be ours.
Through Jesus Christ our healer and friend, Amen.

As we go into the world let us resolve to turn suffering, rejection and loss into strength, compassion and hope.
With God's help we will.

Go in peace to love and serve the Lord.
In the name of Christ, Amen.

⌒

FOR THE HEALING OF THE NATIONS
An Order of Service to Celebrate Creation

Today, we are increasingly aware of the fragility of the planet and the balance of nature. The request by God, in Genesis 28, to 'fill the earth and subdue it' has been mistakenly interpreted as an opportunity to exploit the earth and pollute it, a fact that is particularly obvious to Christians in the Pacific and to indigenous people, such as Native Americans. This 'environmental' order of service draws on prayers and litany from these sources, and from Eco-congregation, the churches' environmental programme. It acknowledges that all God made was good, asks forgiveness for our understanding of 'dominion' over creation, which has damaged the earth, and helps Christians and congregations pledge to do more by offering their own 'green goals' to God.

This liturgy could be used as an alternative to a Harvest Festival service, on 4 October, when St Francis is remembered for his love of animals and nature, or on Conservation Sunday, the first Sunday in June.

Give worshippers pieces of green paper shaped as a leaf as they arrive. In a time of quiet following the reflection, encourage people to write three 'green goals' or environmental pledges on their leaves. These are then attached to a symbol of a bare branched tree during the offering. Discarded tree branches could be used, and arranged in front of the altar, or a drawing of a tree. Leaves may be hung on the branches, or stuck to the tree picture.

The Call to Worship requires symbols of soil, water, a branch, some fruit, a flower and seeds, plus a large candle and several small candles to be brought forward and put in a central position.

CALL TO WORSHIP

In the beginning, God created.
God created the heavens and the earth;
   (*soil*)
light from darkness, day from night;
   (*large candle*)
waters below from waters above, earth from seas;
   (*water*)
lights in the sky – sun and moon and stars.
   (*small candles*)
And God saw that it was good.

Then God spoke and the earth brought forth vegetation;
   (*branch/fruit/flower*)
plants yielding seed of every kind,
trees of every kind bearing fruit with the seed in it.
   (*seeds*)
And God saw that it was good.

And God spoke again, and the waters filled with living
creatures, birds flew in the sky above the earth, the earth
brought forth living creatures, domestic and wild animals of
every kind upon earth.
And God saw that it was good.

Then God spoke into being humankind, male and female
created in the image of God, given dominion over all creation,
filled with the breath, wind, Spirit of the creator.

Pause to listen to your own breathing

**God saw everything that God had made,
and indeed, it was very good.**

God sees us, gathered as the body of Christ throughout this land.
Let us worship our Creator.

Australia

CONFESSION

We confess
that we have considered the earth to be our own,
believing God gave us dominion,
and thus absolute control over it.

We affirm
that, 'the earth is the Lord's and all that is in it,
for he has founded it on the seas
and established it on the rivers.' (Psalm 24.1–2)

We repent.
We know we need to change our
understanding of creation,
taking our share of responsibility for
its care and protection.

We believe
that the spirit, God's recreating power,
is active in us
and in the world.

God, Creator of all,
may humankind be freed from the greed
which is destroying the earth;
And may your churches be courageous
in taking up causes against the forces
that threaten life.
Amen

Fiji

REFLECTION

The prodigal race

There was once a ruler who had two sons. The younger son said
to the ruler: 'Let me have my share of the property.' After a few
days the younger son took his property and got busy, releasing
the assets to create wealth for his use. He dug for coal, drilled for
gas and oil and used the wealth released to go on a spending
spree: fast cars, holidays across the world and every kind of
modern convenience. The more he had, the more he wanted – he
enjoyed every new gadget, unconcerned that the more he used,
the inheritance that he would pass on to his children would
change from a fruitful world to one laid to waste.

If the story ended now, would he come to his senses before it was
too late?

When one machine wore out, another one was ordered and he
amassed more and more, until one day, his oil well ran dry, his

coal was exhausted and he realized he had spent his inheritance and scarred the earth. He sat amid the waste, thinking of the life that those in his father's community once lived, and he wondered if it was too late to say sorry.

Silence

Worshippers are invited to write three environmental promises to God, or 'green goals'. These could be, for example: to recycle cardboard, to reduce heating by one degree, etc.

OFFERING

Leaves are brought forward and attached to a bare branched tree or tree picture

Creator God,
You have promised us a place in your heavenly city,
where the leaves of the tree of life are a medicine for all the
    nations.
Accept these leaves as a sign of our desire to do your will and be
    agents of your healing grace to all the people of the earth, now
    and in the age to come.
Amen.

INTERCESSIONS

Prayers for different elements of the environment – water, trees, plants, air, animals, people, etc. may be said here with the following response, which is adapted from a Native American prayer.

Response to each prayer:

Lord, teach us to walk the soft earth,
As relatives to all that lives.
Give us strength to understand and eyes to see.

AN ENVIRONMENTAL LORD'S PRAYER (with two voices)

Voice 1	*Voice 2*
Our Father who art in heaven	You are also at home in the air, soil, forests and oceans
Hallowed be your name	By the care we take of your creation
Your kingdom come	All that you see is good
Your will be done on earth	Your will to till and care
As it is in heaven.	
Give us this day our daily bread	That all may have sufficient to live life in fullness.
Forgive us our trespasses	Our greed, our exploitation, our lack of concern for other species and for future generations
as we forgive those who trespass against us	by reconciliation with justice and peace
Lead us not into temptation	the temptation to equate dominion with exploitation
And deliver us from evil	the evil of destroying your gift of creation
For yours is the Kingdom	Yours, Lord, not ours
The power and the glory	In the cross and resurrection
For ever and ever	You were the beginning and you are the end.
Amen.	So be it.

FINAL PRAYER

As the air sings with songs of glory,
As the water flashes with the silver of creation,
As the forest blooms with leaves for the healing of nations,
So may God's light and love
Fill our hearts and souls and minds.

A SOUTH INDIAN ORDER OF EVENING PRAYER

Night is falling.
We are preparing to rest.
Let us thank God for the day that is passing.
Let us hold in God's loving presence our concerns
for our world and its people.
Let us be silent.

Silence

How wonderful it is to see your healing presence at work in the
world, restoring your creation moment by moment.
Blessed be God.

How wonderful it is to experience your healing power through
relationships renewed, minds freed and lives made whole.
Blessed be God.

How wonderful it is to feel your healing touch through the
work of doctors and nurses, paramedics and medical
professionals who work with you for the good of others.
Blessed be God.

How wonderful it is to know your healing love through the life
and suffering of our Lord Jesus Christ.
Blessed be God.

How pitiful it is to see your world marred and destroyed by
earthquake and flood, by human selfishness and the misuse of
your good gifts.
Kyrie eleison.

How pitiful it is to encounter lives torn by abusive
relationships, destroyed by drugs, damaged by discrimination
and oppression.
Kyrie eleison.

How pitiful it is for people to know the suffering caused by physical and mental illness, by neglect and by other people's cruelty.
Kyrie eleison.

How pitiful it is to be divided from you by our sinful actions, by our lack of love and by our peace-breaking.
Kyrie eleison.

Let us recognize God's goodness in offering his wholeness and peace to the world and our part in the breaking of that peace. Let us pray.

Short silence

Loving God, whose will is for wholeness for your creation, who seeks to build unity among your troubled and quarrelsome children, we confess our lack of love which damages your world, our lack of care for one another which breaks apart people and nations and families; we come to you for healing and forgiveness. Listen to us as we pray in the name of the one who himself brought unity, healing and peace. Amen.

God who is love forgives us. The one who is peace gives us grace to become peace-makers; the one in whom is healing makes us channels of healing; the one in three who is unity in diversity has made us in his image and calls us to make unity today and always. Blessed be God for ever. Amen.
Halle, halle, hallelujah
Halle, halle, hallelujah
Hallelujah, hallelujah.

PRAYERS OF CONCERN

Let us pray for global peace, especially in the wars and in the violence in many parts of the world.
Kyrie eleison.

Let us pray for our country and the leaders who rule the people. We pray that they might rule with justice and peace to establish a divine society.
Kyrie eleison.

Let us pray for our church. May it strengthen the unity of the churches at large; may it stand as a testimony of oneness of spirit to be a channel of peace in the world.
Kyrie eleison.

Let us pray for our dioceses and their bishops, pastors, missionaries, evangelists, other church workers, hospital staff and teachers. Let them each evaluate their own calling and be truthful in their purpose of that calling.
Kyrie eleison.

Let us remember the departed, their family and friends; may the God of peace console the bereaved ones.
Kyrie eleison.

Let us pray for the churches at large; may they be bridges and channels of peace.
Kyrie eleison.

PRAYER

As you have made this day, O God, you also make the night. Give light for our comfort. Come upon us with quietness and refresh our bodies, that we may listen for the whisper of your Spirit and be attentive to your nearness in our sleep. Empower us to rise again in new life to proclaim your praise, and show Christ to the world, for he reigns for ever and ever. Amen.

THE LORD'S PRAYER

Said in one's own mother tongue

BENEDICTION

Go in peace and sow peace where there is no peace.
May the Triune God make you the channels of peace. Amen.

Jesu supriya,	**Jesus, living Lord,**
Jesu taraka,	**Jesus, strength and stay,**
Jesu priya rakshaka,	**in your mercy bless us all,**
sahaya homala.	**and keep us night and day.**

CHINESE MEDITATIONS FOR CHRISTMAS AND EASTER

ADVENT
Philippians 2.7

But emptied himself

Christ, Son of God, preceded all creation. He is in the image of God, with all of God's majesty, power and glory. Yet he was willing to be humbled, even to be a servant.

It was precisely because he was humbled to the lowest that God exalted him to the highest, above all things. Though he was rich, he became poor for our sake. And because he was poor, God made him heir of all creation.

He cared for neither power nor position, nor did he seek them. He willingly humbled himself, and therefore God filled him with all things. He poured himself out, but God filled him, that all things might find their richness in him.

When will I learn, O God, to see poverty as riches, to see humility as exaltation, to find plenty in emptiness, and empty myself, so that I may be filled with all of creation?

Ambassadors of the Heavenly Kingdom

Ambassadors of the Heavenly Kingdom are called
To save lost souls
And face the sufferings of a long journey.

We wear wind and dust as our clothes,
We walk without staves,
We have no gold or silver in our purses,
We learn from the birds in the sky,
We rely on God for all our needs.

We appear to be poor but we make others rich.
We appear to have nothing,
But we have more than others in every respect.

We commend the new life of Christ,
We advocate the true Gospel of the Cross.
Wherever we go we leave beautiful footprints,
Wherever we go we open the door of grace.

We should lead sinners back to the Lord,
Lead the Prodigal Son to see God the Father.
We do our work with the strength of the Spirit,
Not with our tongues, teeth and lips.
We are ready to sacrifice our lives for the love of others,
Not relying on paper, pens and essays.
We will follow the instructions of the Lord to call the common
    people,
We will respect the Lord's wish to save people from damnation.
Not until the flags of love are planted all over the world
Should we think that we have done our duty.

CHRISTMAS DAY

Luke 2.12

You will find a babe

In the dimness of the stable, faint candlelight glimmers. Under the
lamplight, a newborn babe lies in the manger. Serene, he utters no
cry. Christ has chosen to enter the world, which itself was created
through him.

The first small smile creases his little face. How like the first
Adam. But this small smile also holds a love and obedience which
will meet suffering on the road to the cross.

This small breast, gently rising and falling, is yet boundless
beyond compare. How else could Christ embrace his innumerable
prodigal children who are scattered far and wide? These tiny
shoulders, delicate as jade, are yet strong as metal or stone. How
else could they bear the burden of our human suffering and
concern?

Sleep well, holy infant, may you be wrapped in swaddling
clothes of deep love.

Sleep well, holy infant, there is a manger in my heart for you.

We reverently worship
the mysterious Person, God the Father;

the responding Person, God the Son;
the witnessing Person, the Spirit of Holiness.
We worship the Holy Trinity,
Three persons in one.

I pray that the true God may protect me tonight
Keep me safe from turmoil and trouble.
I pray also for my family and friends,
For all people all over the world –
I pray the cloud of your compassion
May cover them and grant them peace.

EPIPHANY
Matthew 2.1

From the East

Christ, the saviour of humankind, is the great light which shines
upon all peoples. But the very first to be called to worship the holy
infant were the wise men from the East. Why them, in particular?
Was it that the ancient cultures of the East had received more of
God's revelation and were thus better prepared to accept Christ?
Or was it that the East stood in greater need of Christ because of
the endless river of tears which is its history? I do not know.
Perhaps the answer lies in the star that lit their path.

What I do know is that the East, in its recent history, has been
hammered on the anvil of extreme adversity, there forged and
tempered for over a hundred years. Precisely because of this,
should not the East be able to offer up an even more refined gold
when it worships Christ? Out of this pain and agony, should not
the East be ready to bring forth even more fragrant frankincense
and myrrh?

The wise men have already returned home, because people
from the East have a deep sense of attachment to their native
places. And yet, they haven't really gone far from the manger.
Don't you see them still, kneeling over the infant?

From afar you see a high mountain and wonder how you can
ever cross it. But however high the mountain is, you can always
find a pathway over it.

At times our difficulties rise up in front of us like great
mountains, and how can we pass over them? As long as we do not

fear hardship, but walk onwards, a day will surely come when we have overcome them. External barriers cannot block our way forward, it is only despair and weakness in our spirit that can make us falter on the road.

In many cases it is not that the difficulties are insurmountable, but that our own self-imposed limitations make things difficult.

The Lord Jesus has already broken through all the barriers ahead of us. As long as we agree to go forward we can assuredly pass through.

Walk carefully as you go from here
God is there before you.
Walk humbly as you go from here
the churches await your coming.
Walk softly as you go from here
for the Spirit is abroad in all the earth
and the voice of the Spirit speaks in every place.

GOOD FRIDAY
John 19.18

There they crucified him

Who is this man, head crowned with thorns?
   It is my Lord, King of kings, Christ Jesus.
   Why does he carry the cross towards Golgotha?
   He is the sacrificial lamb, led silently to the slaughter.
   Why is this man nailed to a cross on Golgotha?
   He is without sin, yet he dies for us sinners. He bears the sins of
      humankind and is offered up on the sacrificial altar.
   Why does water and blood flow from this man's side?
If blood did not flow, how would my sins be washed away? His blood is the fount of my salvation. And so I kneel at the foot of the cross. The cross is the beginning of my life, and the source to which it returns. The cross is now my life's sign, and its altar.

Bitter cup

Bitter cup, bitter cup,
The bitter cup of the Lord which is hard to drink
Silently obeying the Heavenly Father
Bitterness enters the bone.

In Gethsemane he sweated as if bleeding – for whom?
He bore the pain of whipping – for whom?

He went to death, Cross on back – for whom?
He was butchered like a lamb, without a cry – for whom?

He was deserted by God's people and nailed on the Cross – for
    whom?
In obedience he shed his last drop of blood – for whom?

Bitter cup, bitter cup – for me! for me!

> This is a powerful expression of the years of
> suffering many Chinese Christians have endured.

Help each one of us, gracious God,
to live in such magnanimity and restraint
that the Head of the church
may never have to say of us:
This is my body, broken by you.

EASTER EVE
John 19.42

They laid Jesus there

He was laid in an empty tomb. Just so is a grain of wheat planted
in the ground. The darkness, the cold, the solitude, the bitterness
of death all turned him in the direction of eternal life and a new
day.

If I search carefully in the dark places, I will be able to get a
glimpse of the brilliance which penetrates the whole universe. If I
bend my ear to the silent places, I will be able to hear the thunder
which shakes this vast land. Christ, the Son of God, was willing to
be humbled to the lowest point. He will therefore be raised on
high and receive the praises of all heaven and on earth.

If Christ had not been humbled, how could he be lifted up? If
there were no death, how could there be new life? Without
darkness, how could there be light? Without stillness, how could
we hear sounds?

'Without winter, how could we greet the arrival of spring?'
These are the laws of nature. Are the laws of the spirit any
different?

If I am to suffer, it is for the Lord
My heart will be full of joy, full of joy
I urge the Holy Spirit to hold me on a tight rein
I beg the Holy Spirit to purify my words, deeds and thoughts
Thus I prepare to meet the Lord should I die.

My sufferings were not too long or hard
But they bring unparalleled great glory
If my honour is compared to the humiliations
Contempt, curses and death are of no consequence.

We were fortunate to have prophets like beacons in the dark
The harder the circumstances, the brighter my soul
I beg the Lord for strength to survive a while longer
The one who comes will redress injustice for the innocent.

I should follow the Lord with firm belief
I should bear fruit every day
I should rid myself of sinful thoughts
I should ignore the influence of other people and circumstances
Only seek the favour of the Lord
To take me to paradise when I die.

Fellow Christians are separated by thousands of miles and
    mountain ranges
Separated in body, but we meet in spirit
When the last trumpet is sounded, in an instant
Saints from all times and all places will meet together and never
    part.

A hymn written at the height of the Cultural Revolution

EASTER
Matthew 28.6

He is not here

The stone had been rolled away, and our Lord Jesus Christ had
risen from the dead. He was no longer in the tomb. Neither the
tomb nor death could hold him.

The long night is over. The first rays of the morning sun shine
across the land. Christ is not in the long night. How could the
night hold back the dawn, its morning light breaking through the
rosy clouds?

The opaque shadows have been dispersed, the light of the sun plays upon the tomb. Christ is not in the shadows, for shadows and chill cannot swallow warmth and light!

Of what importance are the sighs and weaknesses of yesterday? Christ does not dwell in weakness or defeat. He is the Lord, now strong and victorious, who rose from the dead.

Why wallow in suffering and despair? Christ dwells not in these things, for he is the Lord, confident and hopeful, who rose from the dead!

Why are we rendered helpless by difficulties? Christ does not dwell in our difficulties and inaction, for he is the Lord of life, the Creator who has risen from the dead!

God, creator of heaven and earth and giver of human life, we thank you for the witness to your truth, your goodness and your beauty which the long history of China has borne. We thank you for the Church in China which is bearing witness to Christ in ways beyond national boundaries. Help us to accept the idea that all local churches are part of your church universal and are witnessing on its behalf and with its blessing. To the glory of Jesus Christ in whom all riches abide. Amen.

Litanies and Prayers

GATHERING/OPENING PRAYERS

1

We come in these moments of quiet to God
Full of all our thoughts and emotions of the day.

We come to still ourselves in God's presence
To reflect and listen and sift through our many ideas.

We come with some faith, and many doubts
We come with our longings and fears and hopes.

We come just as we are
Knowing that God loves us unreservedly.

UK

2

O Lord our God,
Whose righteousness is like the strong mountains
and whose justice is as the great deep:
Let us know your presence now.

O Lord our God,
whose power girds the mountains,
whose hands cradle the hills and yet whose mercy is boundless:
Let us know your presence now.

O Lord our God,
whose glory is greater than our understanding
and whose love cannot be measured:
Let us know your presence now.

UK

3

Jesus, I wish to wait and be ready for your coming
without turning my religious views
or search for well-being

into sedatives.
Help me to believe, love and hope thoroughly.

Brazil

4

We are here as the people of God,
drawn together by his spirit and longing for his word.
We are here to praise the name of the Lord,
to share the glorious news of God's grace,
to pray for our needs and the pains of the world
and to rejoice in his love and his peace.

And as we gather to hear the good news of Christ,
we rejoice in God's unending love for those who are weak and
  vulnerable,
and in the promise of his kingdom of justice.
Yet we recognize that it is our calling to make that kingdom a
  reality;
and we pray that like Christ we may be ready to greet the
  outsider,
uphold the rights of those who suffer injustice,
and seek to change the world through prayer and action.
Heavenly Father, we offer you our praise and worship,
that it may be pleasing to you,
and we offer our lives, that you may use them to fulfil your
  purpose.
We ask these things in the name of your Son,
our Lord and Saviour Jesus Christ.
Amen.

UK

5

O Spirit of Christ, come.
Blaze this darkness among us with your truth.

O Spirit of Peace, come.
Heal our woundedness together.
Amen.

Philippines

6

Come Holy Spirit,
prepare us to change everything that imprisons
the life that comes from you.
Amen.

Brazil

7

Rejoice, people of God!
Celebrate the life within you,
and Christ's presence in your midst!

Our eyes shall be opened!
The present will have new meaning,
and the future will be right with hope.

Rejoice, people of God!
Bow your heads before the One
who is our wisdom and our strength.

We place ourselves before our God.
That we may be touched and cleansed
by the power of God's Spirit.
Amen.

Guatemala

8

A PRAYER FOR ADVENT OR LENT

At Advent (Lent), we should try the key to our heart's door. It
  may have gathered rust.
If so, this is the time to oil it, in order that the heart's door may
  open more easily when the Lord Jesus wants to enter at
  Christmas (Easter) time!
Lord, oil the hinges of our hearts' doors that they may swing
  gently and easily to welcome your coming.

Papua New Guinea

9

In the beginning was God.
In the beginning, the source of all that is.
In the beginning, God yearning,
God moaning,
God labouring,
God giving birth.
God rejoicing!
And God loved what she made.
And God said, 'It is good!'
Then God, knowing that all that is good is shared,
held the earth tenderly in her arms.
God yearned for relationships,
God longed to share the good earth.
And humanity was born
in the yearning of God.
We were born to share the earth.

World Federation of Methodist Women

∽

THANKSGIVING

1

BENEDICITE AOTEAROA

O give thanks to our God who is good:
whose love endures for ever.

You sun and moon, you stars of the southern sky:
give to our God your thanks and praise.

Sunrise and sunset, night and day:
give to our God your thanks and praise.

All mountains and valleys, grassland and scree,
glacier, avalanche, mist and snow:
give to our God your thanks and praise.

You Kauri, and pine, rata and kowhai, mosses and ferns:
give to our God your thanks and praise.

Dolphins and kahawai, sealion and crab,
      coral, anemone, pipi and shrimp:
   give to our God your thanks and praise.

Rabbits and cattle, moths and dogs,
      Kiwi and sparrow and tui and hawk:
   give to our God your thanks and praise.

You Maori and Pakeha, women and men,
      all who inhabit the long white cloud:
   give to our God your thanks and praise.

All you saints and martyrs of the South Pacific:
   give to our God your thanks and praise.

All prophets and priests, all cleaners and clerks,
      professors, shop-workers, typists and teachers,
      job-seekers, invalids, drivers and doctors:
   give to our God your thanks and praise.

All sweepers and diplomats, writers and artists, grocers,
      carpenters, students and stock-agents, seafarers, farmers,
      bakers and mystics:
   give to our God your thanks and praise.

All children and infants, all people who play:
   give to our God your thanks and praise.

Aotearoa/New Zealand

2

Let us give thanks to the beneficent and merciful God, the
father of our Lord God and Saviour, Jesus Christ, for he has
covered us, helped us, guarded us, accepted us to him, spared
us, supported us, and has brought us to this hour. Let us also
ask him, the Lord our God, the Pantocrator [almighty and
omnipotent ruler] to guard us all in peace this holy day and all
the days of our life.

O Master, Lord, God the Pantocrator, the father of our Lord,
God and Saviour, Jesus Christ, we thank you for every
condition, concerning every condition, and in every condition.
For you have covered us, helped us, guarded us, accepted us to
you, spared us, supported us, and brought us to this hour.

Therefore we ask and entreat your goodness, O Philanthropic One [lover of mankind], grant us to complete this holy day, and all the days of our life, in all peace with your fear. All envy, all temptation, all the work of Satan, the counsel of wicked men and the rising up of enemies, hidden and manifest, take them away from us; and from all your people, and from this church and from this holy place that is yours.

But those things which are good and profitable do provide for us, for it is you who have given us the authority to tread on serpents and scorpions, and upon all the power of the enemy.

And lead us not into temptation, but deliver us from evil, by the grace, compassion and philanthropy of your only-begotten Son, our Lord, God and saviour Jesus Christ. Through whom the glory, the honour, the dominion and the adoration are due unto you with him, and the Holy Spirit, the life-giver, who is of one essence with you, now and at all times, and unto the ages of all ages. Amen.

Egypt

3

Red soil, black soil, white sand, yellow clay, brown dirt, glint of gems of every hue, silver, mica, hidden gold.
We give you thanks for the rainbow promise painted in this land.

Bright, dark, dull, blue and grey green of leaves, tiny stars and florid displays, towering kauri, spiky spinifex.
We give you thanks for the kaleidoscope of growth which clothes this land.

Heavy wheat, laden vines, sodden rice, and drying hay, clean, green beef and saltbush mutton, piggeries, fisheries.
We give you thanks for the food coaxed from this land.

Coal for the grid, gas down the pipeline, woodchips and timbers, open cut, underground, in situ leaching and logged, for our way of life, a wealth for the nation.
We give you thanks for the resources of this land offered up for us.

Sole practitioners, teachers on the airwaves, community developers, business, houses and homelands, volunteers, local committees.
We give you thanks that you have made us for community.

Indigenous and immigrant, aged and young, countrymen and countrywomen, caring for family, developing skills, hearts for this land and far lands.
We give you thanks for the peoples of this land, many in heritage, one in future.
We give you thanks, O Creator of all.

Australia

4

A THANKSGIVING FOR HANDS

This meditation was written after the author watched an operation on the hands of a young man, Babu Lal, at the Leprosy Mission Hospital in Naini, South India.

Look for a moment at your hands.

Then think what it would be like if you could not feel:
    the delicacy of a flower,
    the hardness of rock and fragility of an egg shell,
    water splashing through your fingers,
    and sand trickling through your hands,
    lumps of rich brown earth crumbling at your touch,
    sticky clay oozing into random shapes at your squeezing,
    rough woven fabric, prickly wool, cool cotton sheets,
    shiny silks, and soft downy feathers – all different experiences
      of touch.
    All requiring adjustment to pressure to feel their worth.

And the touch of love: perhaps the best of all.
To hold and love, caress and fondle,
fingers entwining in physical pleasure.

The touch of a loving God for our delight.

Now think of the dangers in not being able to feel:
    the prick of a thorn, left to fester,
    the cut of a knife, ignored and not covered,
    scalding water, and burning fire,

blistering skin, inviting infection,
knocks and grazes, unseen or disregarded, too small to notice,
but working their damage on flesh unaware.
Damage to bones overlooked, and unobserved.
The pain of injuries unfelt and unseen.
The gift of pain robbed by leprosy.

The pain of a loving God for our protection.

Look at your hands, look at their beauty and be thankful.

UK/India

⌔

OFFERTORY PRAYERS

1

Lord, use our gifts:
to lighten the darkness of those living in shadows,
to restore dignity to those robbed of their humanity,
to lift the humble and to fill the hungry with good things,
until your kingdom is built with love and justice
and all your people are free.
Amen.

UK

2

Tender God,
who lives in heaven and earth,
in human reason and passion,
you are the holy one in our midst.
Your justice is our peace;
your peace is our hope;
your presence, our delight!
Make our hands, your hands,
our hearts, your heart;
our lives, your life!
Give us this day and always
– a bread of freedom to share,

—62—

– a cup of hope to pour upon the earth.
And may all we do reflect your love for each of us.
All this we ask through Christ, our Saviour. Amen.

UK

3

PRAYER OVER THE BREAD AND WINE

Creator God, give us a heart for simple things:
love and laughter, bread and wine, tales and dreams.
Fill our lives with green and growing hope,
make us a people of justice whose
song is Allelujah and whose name breathes love. Amen.

South Africa

4

Lord God,
whose Son was content to die
to bring new life,
have mercy on your church
which will do anything you ask,
anything at all,
except die
and be reborn.

UK

5

Lord Jesus Christ,
who became poor for our sakes,
grant that we may be transformed to follow your lifestyle
and give to meet the needs of others.
Give us your grace, that,
following in your way,
we may serve instead of expecting to be served,
and accept the challenge of your life
given as a ransom for all.
Amen.

India

6

God of hope and joy,
in your greatness you call us
to seek those who are lost,
forgotten and isolated.

God of light and strength,
by your grace
you call us to be together
to journey our understanding of the way.

Show us the way forward
into this world you love,
to be your hands and heart,
to respond with willingness and humility,
to love and share
as you have loved and shared.

Send us to the edges,
give us the grace to stand beside
those who are voiceless,
marginalized and rejected,
those who experience pain and hardship,
loneliness and grief, coldness and hunger.

Show us how to care, how to listen,
how to respond, how to love,
how to proclaim and liberate.

Lead us so that in being
your hands and heart,
we may ever faithfully
walk in your spirit.
Amen.

Australia

7

There's a time for healing,
and a time for forgiving.
There's a time for building bridges,
and that time is now.

O, take our hearts, Lord,
take our minds.
Take our hands, Lord,
and make them one.
Amen.

Israel

8

Servant-Christ, help us to follow you in untiring ministry to town and village, to heal and restore the broken body of humanity, to cast out the demonic forces of greed, resentment, communal hatred and self-destructive fears;
Servant-Christ, help us all to follow you.

Help us to follow you on the road to Jerusalem, to set our faces firmly against friendly suggestions to live a safe, expedient life; to embrace boldly the way of self-offering, the way of life given for others' gain;
Servant-Christ, help us all to follow you.

Help us to follow you into the temple of your chosen people to share your meal of bread and cup, to accept our common place in your one body broken to create a new humanity.
Servant-Christ, help us all to follow you.

Help us to follow you into the garden, to watch with you, ever vigilant for signs of the dawning of your day, to struggle unsparingly, to understand and to be obedient to your perfect will.
Servant-Christ, help us all to follow you.

Help us to follow you unto the cross, to recognize the true way of life in your death, to see our hope in your self-spending love to die to all within us not born of your love.
Servant-Christ, help us all to follow you.

Help us to follow you out of the dark tomb; to share daily in your resurrection life, to be renewed daily in your image of love, to serve daily as your new body in ministering to the world.
Servant-Christ, help us all to follow you.

India

9

PRAYER FOR OPENNESS, WITH ACTIONS

God my creator   *(hands folded in praying position on the chest)*

I open my heart to you   *(hands shaped like a heart)*
May it turn to you   *(hands turned upwards)*
As the sunflower turns to the   *(eyes and face follow hands)*
  sun.

God my redeemer   *(hands folded in prayer)*
Take away from my heart   *(open hands in supplication)*
Everything that is not love   *(hands folded with thumbs pointing to heart)*

So that I may reach out
To you in my own
  unworthiness.   *(hands raised with palms upwards)*

God my sanctifier   *(hands folded in prayer)*
Journey with me along life's
  way   *(open hands in supplication)*
So that all that I am   *(hands towards the heart)*
And all that I do   *(hands move slowly upwards, palms up)*

May bring greater glory to you   *(hands make a full circle and come down slowly)*

the triune God. Amen.   *(hands back in prayer position)*

Sri Lanka

10

Give us courage, O Lord, to stand up and be counted,
to stand up for those who cannot stand up for themselves,
to stand up for ourselves when it is needful for us to do so.
Let us fear nothing more than we fear you.
Let us love nothing more than we love you,
for thus we shall fear nothing also.
Let us have no other God before you,
whether nation, or party, or state, or church.
Let us seek no other peace but the peace which is yours,
and make us its instruments,
opening our eyes and our ears and our hearts,

so that we should know always what work of peace we may do
for you.

South Africa

༄

AFFIRMATIONS OF FAITH

1

We believe in God who loves us
and wants us to love each other.
This is our God.

We believe in Jesus who cared
about children and held them in his arms.
He wanted a world where everyone
could live together in peace.
This is Jesus Christ.

We believe in the Holy Spirit who
keeps working with us until
everything is good and true.
This is the Holy Spirit.

We can be the church which reminds
people of God because we love each other.
This we believe.
Amen.

Prepared by children for the
World Council of Churches' Assembly in Canberra

2

I believe in the equality of all,
rich and poor.
I believe in liberty.
I believe in humanity and that through it
we can create unity.
I believe in the love within each of us,
and in the home, happy and healthy.

I believe in the forgiveness of our sins.
I believe that with divine help
we will have the strength to establish
equality in society.
I believe in unity, the only way to achieve peace,
and I believe that together we can obtain justice.
Amen.

Peru

3

We believe in God,
the creator of all life and beauty,
who blesses our journey.

We believe in Jesus Christ,
who lived as a friend and saviour to all he met
as he travelled the countryside,
who ate and laughed,
wept and celebrated with people in all walks of life.

We believe in the Holy Spirit,
who rides on the breeze in the country
touching all with gentleness and love;
who strengthens our commitment,
who offers us eternal hope.

We believe in the church,
which stands open to all travellers
and bears witness to the everlasting love of God.

Australia

CONFESSION AND ABSOLUTION

1

God, our Creator, who has made us your human children as
one family in you, so that what concerns any must concern all,
we confess the evils we have done and the good we have left
undone.

We have spent our strength too often upon the tower of Babel of our own pride, and have forgotten the city that has foundations, whose builder and maker is you.

We have been content that we ourselves should prosper though many might be poor, that a few should feast while multitudes were famished both in body and in soul.

O you, who has taught us that whatsoever we sow, we shall also reap, help us to repent before your judgement comes.

Silence

For the clouded eyes that see no further than our own advantage:
We confess our sins, O God.

For the dulled imagination that does not know what others suffer:
We confess our sins, O God.

For the willingness to profit by injustice which we have not striven to prevent:
We confess our sins, O God.

For the selfishness that is quick to gain and slow to give:
We confess our sins, O God.

For the unconcern that makes us cry, 'Am I my brother's keeper?'
We confess our sins, O God.

You, who are ever merciful, take away the evil of our conscious and unconscious wrong, forgive us for our unfaithfulness to the vision of your Kingdom, and grant to us a better purpose for the days to come.

From acquiescence in old iniquities:
Save us, O God.

From indifference to the human cost of anything we covet:
Save us, O God.

From the greed that wastes the lives of men and women through unemployment, poverty and deprivation:
Save us, O God.

From the cruelty that exploits the needy and defenceless:
Save us, O God.

From false leadership in business, government and in the church:
Save us, O God.

Unless the Lord builds the house
our labour is in vain.
But the One that sits upon the throne said,
'Behold, I make all things new.'

Even so, O God, let your redemptive purposes work through us
to build a new and better order on this earth, for the blessing of
your people and the glory of your name, through Jesus Christ.
Amen.

USA

2

Jesus, may we never forget that you lived your life as a Jew;
and in the remembering
free us from the temptation to despise the cultures of others.
Show us the way to tolerance,
mutual learning,
and an appreciation of what unites us as people.

UK

3

O Lord, you created us equal; yet we have treated one another
unjustly.
Forgive us, O God.

You created us in your holy image. Yet we have failed to
recognize the dignity and sacredness of your image in every
person.
Forgive us, O God.

Some of the old wounds of injustice are still bleeding, and our
scars prevent us from being as sensitive to others as we ought
to be.
Heal us, O God.

Help us to hear your cry in the cries of others and feel your
pain in their pain.
Help us, O God.

As the new, tender skin emerges from under the old scars, create in us a new humanity through the brokenness of our experiences.
Create in us, O God, a new humanity.

May we celebrate together the dignity and sacredness of humanity in one another and for the sake of your glory.
For the sake of your glory.
Amen.

USA

4

A journey is not easy. Our journey together has not been easy.

To move from sin into wholeness is risky, painful, filled with peril. We have met obstacles on the way and we have found resistance in our own soul.

Some of us have heard the call, but have worked hard to keep others from hearing. Others have acknowledged the call for all but wanted to keep some 'in their place' on the journey. Others of us have heard the call but are afraid of what it means. Like Jonah, we have tried to run the other way.

Still others of us have started out, but like the children of Israel in the Exodus, the journey has become hard, and we have wanted to turn back to our place of captivity. We looked for the security of the days when everyone knew their own place.

All of these obstacles are the sin of racism.
Racism is a barrier.
Racism is a burden.
Racism interrupts God's call.
Racism destroys God's community.
Racism is a cancer in the souls of God's people –
and God's judgement on racism is clear.

To keep on the journey we need to know about the sin of racism and we need to turn to God and to one another in repentance.
God of mercy, we acknowledge the sin of racism, we have not been what you have called us to be. We have wounded the body of Christ, even as we have wounded those persons whom you have called to share in your grace. Forgive us our sin and lead us

into new life through the one who was broken for us, Jesus
Christ, your Chosen One, our Saviour.
Amen.

USA

5

Dear God, the waters that wash the shores of our islands remind
us that your Spirit is moving over our region.

Forgive us for not taking good care of the resources of the sea.
In our indifference, we pollute by casting off waste – disused
cans, bottles, sticks, oil, any and everything into the waters.

Help us to become a people who take greater pride in what you
have entrusted to us.

May we ever strive to make you proud of us. Help us work
towards the time when our waters challenge us to the need for
cleanliness in every sphere of existence.

As your son called people who made a living by the waters to
follow him, so may we hear your voice beckoning us to serve
you.
Amen.

Caribbean

6

Right side   We have marred your image within us, O God, for we
have violated the spirit of love which you intended for
each of us to express.

Left side   You have called us to be sisters and brothers together,
taking responsibility for your creation.

Right side   But we have divided ourselves by the erection of
barriers of superiority and power; by not encouraging
people to develop pride in themselves which is theirs
as children of God.

Left side   We have glorified ourselves at the expense of the
dignity and humanity of others.

Right side   Sometimes, O God, we have lived, and taught our
children to live, by a creed of racism, declaring that

some of us, by reason of our colour, are superior and others of us are inferior. And what is more, O God, we have developed ways to institutionalize our racial sins against one another and to justify them in your name.

Left side We have forgotten the partnership of our creation and denied each other equal places of honour and responsibility within the world, forgetting that no one of us can make it on our own, but we need each other.

Right side At times, O God, we have abused our children and battered our old, forgetting that people of all ages are sacred.

Left side By our insensitivity to justice, we have removed from our sight the presence of those who are poor, hurting, broken, marginalized and imprisoned.

Right side We confess unto you, O God, that there is a sickness within us and there is a brokeness within our community.

Left side Because we have not recognized the presence of your Christ in the faces and conditions of our sisters and brothers, we have sinned against you.

Right side We cry out for healing: 'Is there no balm in Gilead, is there no great physician there?'

Left side Hear our prayer, O God, and forgive us, we pray.

All **Hear not simply the recitation of our offences, but see also the sorrow of our hearts.**
Forgive our sins of racism, which we have confessed unto you.
Give unto us newness of life and singleness of heart, that we may perform the intentions which we speak silently with you.
This we ask through Christ our crucified and risen Saviour.
Amen.

USA

—73—

7

When the church prefers to worship success
rather than see God's grandeur in the small:
Then will Jesus say: 'Let the children come.'

When the church craves its own importance,
becoming too busy for laughter:
Then will Jesus say: 'Let the children come.'

When the church seeks to silence the voices of its children,
finding the exuberance of youth too discordant:
Then will Jesus say: 'Let the children come.'

When the church is fearful of human sorrow,
because it cannot provide all the answers:
Then will Jesus say: 'Let the children come.'

When the church cannot bear to be adventurous,
choosing sterility rather than risking mistakes:
Then will Jesus say: 'Let the children come.'

When the church is so eager to speak,
that it forgets the call to listen:
Then will Jesus say: 'Let the children come.'

When the church makes an idol of the past,
because it dreads the challenge of the future:
Then will Jesus say: 'Let the children come.'

UK

8

*A candle may be lit at the end of each stanza, or the prayer divided so
each stanza is used at a different point in the service.*

Wondrous and holy God,
Creator of the universe,
you make all people
in your own image,
you live and work in our midst.
You bless us
with an immense variety of cultures and
ways of responding to you.
You show us new patterns

of living and loving in Jesus.
You give us strength
by your Holy Spirit.
We bless and thank you.

Forgive us when we
put boundaries around
your presence, love and work;
when we use diversity to divide people –
to demonize some and
accord privileged status to others;
when we seek to dominate or destroy those who are different.
Have mercy on us.

Show us all how to
live and work with others;
to receive diversity as a gift
and not as a threat;
to move beyond tolerance of
those who are different
to mutual respect and trust.
Show us the art of listening
with respect
to one another.
Grant us the help of your spirit,
that in humility
we may share with others
our faith and story.
In the name of Christ
Amen.

UK

9

I am ashamed before the earth;
I am ashamed before the heavens;
I am ashamed before the evening twilight;
I am ashamed before the blue sky;
I am ashamed before the darkness;
I am ashamed before the sun;
I am ashamed before the One standing within me who speaks to me.

The Navaho, Canada

10

POLES APART – TOGETHER IN CHRIST
Part 1

This can be prayed using several voices. Part 2 can be found on page 94.

Voice 1   'As the heavens are higher than the earth, so are my ways higher than your ways and my thoughts than your thoughts.' (Isaiah 55.9)

Voice 2   As the north pole is distant from the south, so far are our ideals, our visions and our hopes from your creative plan.

Voice 3   As the south pole is remote from the north, so far are our mediocre achievements from our modest aspirations.

Voice 1   A yawning abyss divides us from you and from one another:

Voice 2   our narrow horizons –

Voice 3   your world-embracing passion;

Voice 2   our obsession with comfort –

Voice 3   your purpose of wholeness;

Voice 2   our compromised search for peace –

Voice 3   your perfect shalom.

Voice 1   Your thoughts and ours: poles apart.
Our ways and yours: a world of difference.

All   **God, in your mercy, forgive what we are and draw us closer to you.**

Pardon

Voice 1   'As the heavens are high above the earth, so great is God's steadfast love ... As far as the east is from the west, so far God removes our transgressions from us.' (Psalm 103.11–21)

Voice 2   Your love encircles the equator; your mercy stretches from pole to pole.

Voice 3   Your redeeming grace bridges the abyss, and draws us to you.

Voice 2   Yet your children remain at odds; your creation is dislocated.

Voice 3   Reconcile us to one another and to you. Relocate us in one world-wide community of love.

All   **Thanks be to God for the reality of our forgiveness and the promise of our renewal.**

UK

11

We acknowledge our responsibility
for sin and evil,
in the world,
in our country,
in our work-places,
in our homes and schools,
in our temples and churches.
We acknowledge our want of faith, hope and love.

We acknowledge our pride, vanity and self-indulgence.
We acknowledge our selfishness and narrowness of spirit and our exploitation of others.

We acknowledge our failures and omissions in the care and service of others.
We acknowledge divisions among us, and failures and omissions in corporate action for justice for the oppressed.

We need cleansing and forgiveness and humility of spirit.
We need new life, true community and real joy.
We need liberation, reconciliation and peace.

Silence

We seek to change our lives and to change the organization of society.
In order to help build a new society and a new humanity, a new heaven and a new earth.
We seek a revolution of mind and spirit, a revolution in the structures of society,

a revolution in human relationships between
leaders and people, administrators and workers,
teachers and pupils, parents and children, priests and laity.

We seek liberation for all those who are oppressed.
We seek to commit ourselves to the struggle for liberation.

We seek a new order of love, justice and peace that all may care.
**We seek sharing of power and resources of leadership and
responsibility.**
**We seek day by day, to translate principles into practice as far as
we can, alongside the people, according to dharma.**

Sri Lanka

12

Gracious God, when we are tormented by thoughts
of our past guilt,
bring to our minds that you have already
blotted out and forgotten it.
When we feel that we are tainted by dirt and filth all around,
let us feel washed by the torrent of your pardoning love.
When we are tempted to swell in self-righteousness,
remind us of how we fail to fulfil your commandments of love.
Just like the wiper of the windscreen wipes away the splashing
water, let us feel that your grace overcomes our faults at every
    moment.
Make us sensitive so that we will avoid that which will grieve
    you,
and help us to seek always to do your will.
In the name of the one who never turned away anyone who came
    to him,
even Jesus Christ your Son and our Saviour.
Amen.

India/UK

〜

INTERCESSIONS

1

O Tree of Calvary,
send your roots deep down
into my heart.
Gather together the soil of my heart,
the sands of my fickleness,
the mud of my desires.
Bind them all together,
O Tree of Calvary,
interlace them with your strong roots,
entwine them with the network
of your love.
Amen.

India

2

PRAYER-FATIGUE

The shouts are too loud.
They so often deafen my ears.
War, famine, destruction, death –
the sufferings of the world glide past my soul.
I have heard too much to care.

But then you, O God,
you stand in the midst of the world's woe,
and the shapes of those who suffer are no longer faceless,
for you have bequeathed to them your own face,
their pain is etched with the lines of your passion.
And I shall proclaim: 'I had heard, but now I see.'

The people are too many.
They blur together in my imagination.
Races, colours, faiths and languages –

their shifting kaleidoscope dazzles my vision.
I am made giddy by their infinite variety.

But then you, O God,
you are the still point around which all revolves,
in you both light and shadow find an equilibrium:
you paint into life our many-peopled world,
your love refracts us into a rainbow of hope.
And I shall proclaim: 'I had heard, but now I see.'

UK

3

A PRAYER FOR INDIA

Dear God,

We remember the great nation of India. We thank you for all
that it represents in beauty, colour, and diversity – of the land,
its peoples, its languages, and especially the vibrant faith of
many different persuasions.

In the name of religion the embers of hatred and violence are
stirred against those who have chosen to follow Christ's way.
We pray that you will intervene.

Call to reason those set on the path of militancy, challenge the
leaders of the nation to staunchly uphold the rights of all
minorities which its Constitution enshrines.

Bless your Church, that it may be strengthened and given
courage in adversity; that it may not betray its call to be faithful
to Christ's call of witnessing and reconciling discipleship.
Amen.

Germany/India

4

O Lord Jesus Christ, strengthen the love and commitment
of your people in Jerusalem and the Middle East
in this time of uncertainty and challenge.
Let them never forget your promises:
'Peace I leave with you; my peace I give to you,'
and
'Do not let your hearts be troubled, and do not let them be afraid.'

We pray for peace, with justice, for the wounded
and broken-hearted, and dignity to be restored to all.

Pray not for Arab or Jew,
for Palestinian or Israeli.

But pray for yourselves,
that you may not divide them
in your prayers,
but keep them together
in your hearts.

Palestine

5

A PRAYER FOR CHINA

Crowded on subways,
labouring on building sites,
toiling in rice-fields,
serving in shops,
working in factories
teaching in schools,
relaxing in pool halls,
lounging on streets,
training for Olympics,
computing in offices,
governing in ministries,
trading in markets,
performing in theatres,
strolling in parks,
praying in temples,
exercising, chatting, cycling, cooking,
eating, learning, loving, burying ...
behold the people of China – your people.

We pray for their health and safety,
for the conscientious management of all workplaces.
We pray for economic and judicial systems
where neither rewards nor punishments are excessive.
We pray that rulers and people alike may be free of both fear and
    greed

and for peaceful international partnership with China in all walks
of life.

We ask God's blessing
on the churches throughout China, including Hong Kong;
on over-stretched and under-resourced pastors;
on those who define and refine,
test and contest the relations between church and state.

UK – Friends of the Church in China

6

God, what kind of world is this,
that the adult people are going to leave for us children?
There is fighting everywhere
and they tell us we live in a time of peace.
You are the only one who can help us.
Lord, give us a new world,
in which we can be happy,
in which we can have friends,
and work together for a good future.
A world in which there will not be any cruel people
who seek to destroy us and our world
in so many ways.
Amen.

Liberia

7

Dear God, our Father and our Mother,
we thank you that you are the God of compassion and justice;
for your promise to turn darkness into light.
We pray for places where darkness prevails,
for political prisoners who are away from their homelands;
for countries where people experience instability and exploitation
because of the involvement of foreign powers.
We pray that you will bring justice and peace to them.

India

8

We remember those who live in lands of drought or flood,
whose harvest is inadequate or non-existent.
Today they sow in tears:
may they soon reap with shouts of joy.

We remember those whose water supply is polluted, by
    negligence or need,
those to whom water brings disease, poisoning or radiation – the
    curse of death rather than the gift of life.
Today they sow in tears:
may they soon reap with shouts of joy.

We remember ourselves, our waste of water, our profligacy with
    the fruits of the earth,
our unwillingness to be bound together as one with our brothers
    and sisters throughout the world.
May we learn to share their tears:
that soon we may all reap with shouts of joy.

UK

9

A BIBLICAL LITANY OF AND FOR MOTHERS

Eve, mother of our humanity:
Teach us true wisdom, that all life is precious in God's eyes.

Sarah, Hannah and Elizabeth, yearning for a child:
Comfort and strengthen all who know the pain of infertility.

Hagar, condemned to the harshness of exile:
Sustain those who struggle to feed their sons and daughters.

Rebecca, bride from a far-off land:
Welcome women who must bring up a family among strangers.

Rachel, weeping for your children:
Weep with all mothers whose children have disappeared.

Jochebed, mother of Moses and Miriam:
**Lend your ingenuity to women who seek protection for their
    children.**

Naomi and Ruth, bound together by a love greater than blood:
Show us how bitter disappointment can become the sweetness of hope.

Mary, daughter of Israel, mother of Jesus:
Share with us God's secrets that you have pondered deep within your heart.

UK

10

Lord, we cannot properly reflect on the meaning of the cross
while life is easy and comfortable.
Let us follow you on your way to Golgotha
again and again, bearing the pain and sin of humanity,
yet directing all our deep questions to you, you alone.
Loving God, you create and recreate;
you allow all things to die and you bring to life.
Let us not aspire to glory without suffering,
confidence without self-denial,
or eternal life without dying.

India

11

We pray:
For our nation, our neighbours, our congregation,
for ourselves and our families,
for those we have loved but see no more,
for all Christ's people, the community of God's love:
Let us pray to the Lord.
Lord, hear our prayer.

For those who are weary from serving humanity,
for those who are doubtful of serving God,
for those who are fearful of their inadequacy:
Let us pray to the Lord.
Lord, hear our prayer.

For those who don't know what to believe,
who cannot believe, who refuse to believe,
for those who believe but whose unbelief needs help:
Let us pray to the Lord.
Lord, hear our prayer.

Through Christ who suffered for us,
through Christ who conquered death for us,
through Christ who rose in glory for us:
Let us pray to the Lord.
Lord, hear our prayer.

Glory to the Father who saves us,
and to the Son who forgives and heals us,
and to the Holy Spirit who gives us life:
As it was in the beginning,
is now, and ever shall be,
world without end.
Amen.

UK

12

Lord, how realistically do we pray
'Thy will be done on earth as it is in heaven'?
At what cost to ourselves?

Ireland

13

PRAYING WITH CHRISTIANS IN CHINA

Let us pray, holding memories, images and people before God:

For those we know in China: may they have the joy of the sun
clearing the morning mist and the tasks before them; the joy of
the evening moon reflected in water, sign of a day's work well
done.

For those in the Chinese Church in places and times of tension
and strife: that the healing peace of the high hills of this earth
and the Spirit may come to them.

For those whose road has been paved with the ice of bitterness
and hardship: that the warm sun of God's love may clear the
path.

For the women of China, especially the old, bowed in prayer,
the trees of the church that have come through storms, the sap
of their spirit still rising in their hearts and hands.

For those whose have lost their bearings in the forest and their foothold in the marsh: may they find a new path lit by Christ's lantern, with firm ground underfoot.

For ourselves, that we may be open to new visions of what the will of God is for all Christians, in China and our own land: that we may climb from the narrow familiar valleys of our homes to see from high the glory of the many-coloured landscape of God's realm.
Amen.

UK – Friends of the Church in China

14

We pray for a new vision which includes the poor,
the exploited, the marginal, those in need
and those without voice and power.

We thank God for renewed efforts
to advocate rights of community
and care of the environment;
for opposition to the dumping of nuclear and toxic waste in the
    Pacific;
for international moves to curb greenhouse gas emissions;
for a response from industrialized countries
to the plea of the Pacific Conference of Churches
for respect for the integrity of a fragile environment.

May the Pacific become the ocean of peace,
and of spiritual and economic significance for island peoples.
Amen.

Fiji

15

PSALM OF THE PACIFIC
You who turn storms into gentle winds,
and troubled seas into tranquil waters,
you who make yams grow
and bananas blossom,
wash our people with justice;
teach us with righteousness;

speak to us daily;
strengthen us to serve you.

Papua New Guinea

16

A RESPONSIVE LORD'S PRAYER

Our Father in Heaven,
**Remind us constantly that you are parent to all your children,
whoever, or wherever they are or come from.**

Hallowed be your name.
Your Kingdom come,
Establishing peace and justice, hope and life for all peoples.

Your will be done on earth as it is in heaven.
Give us today our daily bread.
Disturb us into awareness of the needs of others.

Forgive us our sins,
Our pride and our prejudices.

As we forgive those who sin against us.
Lead us not into temptation,
**Especially keep our hearts and minds open
to see the good in others.**

Deliver us from evil.
For the kingdom,
Just and true,

The power,
Gentle and fair,

And the glory,
Shot through with the colours of love,

Are yours for ever and ever.
Amen.

UK

17

Inspired by the words of Teresa of Avila: 'Pray as you can, for prayer doesn't consist of thinking a great deal, but of loving a great deal.'

Loving God, we seek your way. We pray as we can:
For those who are our care, and who care for us.
Our worries and our responsibilities, but also our joys and
   delights.
For those dear to us, for good friends, for those on whom we rely.

Loving God, we seek your way. We pray as we can:
For those alongside whom we minister.
For all who share the tasks of ministry, and the urgencies of
   mission.
For those whose company we enjoy, and for those with whom we
   have less sympathy or mutual regard.
For the church in her disagreements and disputes.
Show us the route to reconciliation.

Loving God, we seek your way. We pray as we can:
For a troubled world, where thoughts of vengeance and rage
   come so much easier than belonging and wide compassion.
Teach us how to pray for our enemies.
Show us the path to life for all your people.

Loving God, we seek your way. We pray as we can:
For individuals in trouble or pain.
For the hungry, the war-weary, the desperate.
Widen our sympathy, make our love grow.

UK

18

PRAYER FOR INTER-FAITH UNDERSTANDING
Immeasurable God, creator and father of all humans,
we marvel at the immense variety of cultures and religious
   traditions.
We are perplexed by conflicting truth-claims and competing
   interests.
We are overwhelmed by the complexity,
and confused by the contradictions.

Help us to transcend our self-imposed limitations,
and be open to your future.
Motivate us to join with people of other faiths in friendship and
    with mutual trust,
standing together on common interests and complementary
    concerns.
Where our words fail, make our silence genuine and reflective.
Whatever way we turn in the journey of dialogue
in Christ with others,
let us not deviate from your greatest command of loving you with
    all our being,
and loving others as ourselves.
Through your son and in the fellowship of the guiding Spirit.
Amen.

India

19

FOR THOSE OF US DYING OF AIDS

O God of love,
whose mercy has always included those who are forgotten,
those who are isolated and those who suffer,
bless, we beseech you, all of us who are afflicted by HIV and
    AIDS.
Comfort us in our pain, sustain us in our days of hopelessness,
and receive us into the arms of your mercy in our dying.
Open people's hearts to provide for our needs,
to take away our isolation,
to share our journey of suffering and sorrow,
and to be present with us so we need not die alone.
Bless those of us who mourn the death of our friends and lovers;
may we not be overwhelmed by death,
but receive comfort and strength to meet the days ahead
with trust and hope in your goodness and mercy.
Amen.

South Africa

20

PRAYER FOR A CURE FOR AIDS

O blessed Lord Jesus Christ,
whose name is given for health and salvation,
enlighten with the spirit of wisdom and knowledge those
  researchers, scientists and technicians who seek a cure for AIDS
  and its related conditions;
be present with them in their perplexity,
and, at last, prosper their efforts with such success that those who
  were without hope may rejoice,
and those who were considered dead may be raised up.
In the name of the one who lives and reigns with the Father and
  the Holy Spirit,
one God for ever and ever. Amen.

South Africa

21

Creator God,
gentle in power and strong in tenderness:
kindle, we pray, in the hearts of all people
your passion for peace and your will for justice,
that we may fearlessly contend against the powers of death
and restrain evil's rage with your love.
Heal us and teach us your ways in this hour.
In Jesus' name. Amen.

UK

⮌

ADORATION AND PRAISE

1

Great is, O King,
our happiness
in thy kingdom,
thou, our King.

We dance before thee,
our King,
by the strength
of thy kingdom.
May our feet
be made strong,
let us dance before thee,
eternal.

Give ye praise,
all angels,
to him above
who is worthy of praise.

Traditional Zulu, South Africa

2

LIFETIME PSALM

Praise my soul our good Lord,
sing songs to his name,
for he has brought my life
into fresh waters when I was thirsty.
He has fed me with the Bread of Life
when I was starving.
He has sustained me along all my days
and never has put me to shame.
Praise my soul our good Lord,
for all his goodness.

Uruguay

3

A MOTHER'S PSALM

Give praise for the gift of children,
for the birth of love
and the blessings of laughter and joy and rollicking music.
Sing out to God,
who from the shadows of pain
gives birth to life anew.
Celebrate.
For with the ravines and lonely valleys

—91—

comes the warm wind
and the life-giving rain.

Sierra Leone

4

Lord, you beat in our hearts and are present
in every cell of our bodies,
all that we are leaps for delight,
wherever we go, we know we shall find you there.

Nicaragua

5

With people of every time and place, we offer God the gift of
praise as we ask that our love be made wide enough to include
all peoples.
In this spirit we cry out:
Praise to you, O God of Life.

We worship God, who has enriched the fabric of our lives with
the diversity of every race and culture, as we cry out:
Praise to you, O God of Life.

We praise the God who continually calls us to put aside the
weapons of hatred and discrimination, as we cry out:
Praise to you, O God of Life.

We adore the God who makes the rain to refresh us in our
common labours for justice and peace, as we cry out:
Praise to you, O God of Life.

We praise the God who has fashioned us to be the one Body of
Christ, proclaiming the one gospel, as we cry out:
Praise to you, O God of Life.

We adore the God who has called us to give proud witness to
the unity and diversity of human hearts enlightened beyond the
dark power of discrimination, as we cry out:
Praise to you, O God of Life.

We are filled with joy for those in our midst whose courageous
love has called each of us beyond the sinfulness of hatred and
prejudice, as we pray:
Praise to you, O God of Life.

We are filled with joy at the presence of the Risen Shepherd, who calls us from our divisions to a new unity of mind and heart, as we cry out:
Praise to you, O God of Life.

We indeed give God praise and thanks for this time together, for calling us to be a new creation, bringing about the reconciliation of Christ to a broken world.
We give praise to you, O God of Life, now and for ever. Amen.

USA

6

Voice 1   If only we had been there
when the earth was born,
perhaps we would have seen more clearly
how precious is our world, how fragile and
irreplaceable,
perhaps we might have cherished it better and loved it
more.

Voice 2   If only we had been there
when the morning stars sang together,
and the holy ones shouted for joy.

Voice 1   If only we had been there
when the vast cathedral of the skies first soared aloft,
perhaps the music of the stars
would have soothed our spirits,
and played their harmonies into the lyrics of our lives,
perhaps we too might have learned by heart the great
psalms of peace.

Voice 2   If only we had been there
when the morning stars sang together,
and the holy ones shouted for joy.

Voice 1   If only we had been there
when people could meet God face to face,
in garden or in whirlwind,
perhaps it would have been easier to live with questions,
knowing God didn't want us to stop asking them,
perhaps we might have understood they can't all be
answered – at least this side of eternity –

Voice 2 If only we had been there
when the morning stars sang together,
and the holy ones shouted for joy.

Voice 1 If only we had been there
when the lamb was offered before the world's
    foundation,
perhaps we would have grasped God's perfect pattern,
how love and sacrifice are woven into the fabric of the
    universe,
perhaps we too might have learned obedience,
treading the way of the servant Son.

Voice 2 If only we had been there
when the morning stars sang together,
and the holy ones shouted for joy.

UK

7

POLES APART – TOGETHER IN CHRIST
Part 2

This can be prayed using several voices. Part one can be found on page 76.

Voice 1 'Many will come from east and west, from north and south, and sit down at the feast in the kingdom of God.' (Luke 13.29)

Voice 2 Toiling over freezing mountain passes; struggling across trackless deserts; in leaking boats on stormy seas: let them come.

Voice 3 From cathedral and chapel, gurdwara and synagogue, mosque and temple: let them come.

Voice 2 Let them sit and find rest; let them eat and be filled; let them feast and rejoice and let God's kingdom come.

Voice 3 Then shall the wisdom of the east and the insight of the west, the vision of the south and the knowledge of the north all combine;

Voice 2 Then shall the might of the west and the energy of the east, the power of the north and the strength of the south unite;

Voice 1	and the world shall know peace and harmony and joy; for God's kingdom has come.
Voice 2	And the nations of the south shall bring their worship,
Voice 3	and the clans of the west shall bring their praise,
Voice 2	and the tongues of the north their songs of gladness,
Voice 3	and the peoples of the east their adoration.
All	**O give thanks to the Lord, for he is good; for his steadfast love endures for ever.**
Voice 1	'Let the redeemed of the Lord say so, those who have been redeemed from trouble and gathered in from the east and from the west, from the south and from the north.' (Psalm 107.1–3)
All	**This is God's promise.** **This is Christ's purpose.** **This is our destiny.** **Alleluia! Amen!**

UK

⌐

BENEDICTIONS/CLOSING PRAYERS

1

The blessings of the Lord are with us.
Jesus' love is also with us.
The spirit of unity is also with us.
Let us go bravely into the world
to fight a good fight for Justice and Truth.

Dalits, once known as the Untouchables, India

2

May you know the peace
of the One who stills the tempest;
may you know the comfort

of the One who gives sweet rest;
may you know the power
of the One from whom demons cower;
may you know the joy
of the One who welcomes sinners;
may you know the victory
of the One who conquered the grave;
may you know the new life
of the One who alone can save.
Amen.

Caribbean

3

God came down to us
like the sun at morning
wounded to the heart
by our helplessness.
Let us now depart
in his strength
to love and serve
one another.

India

4

Everlasting God, your son Jesus Christ has sent us into the world
    to preach the gospel of his kingdom.
Raise up in this and every land
heralds and evangelists of your kingdom,
that your church may make known the immeasurable riches of
    our Saviour Christ,
who lives and reigns with you and the Holy Spirit,
one God, now and for ever. Amen.

UK

5

Almighty and most loving God,
we acknowledge your overflowing love and infinite glory.
Purify our hearts,
teach us how to love and forgive.

Pour down on us the spirit of peace and reconciliation.
Challenge us to go out in service:
to transform the world through self-renewal,
to transform suffering into commitment,
to transform confusion into creativity,
to transform death into life.
Teach us how to proclaim the good news:
that we may be instruments of justice,
committed to peace and equality for all.
Teach us, your people, how to survive amid death by starvation,
misery and destitution,
torture and disappearance.
Lord, sometimes our faith trembles.
Lord, sometimes it seems as though you have left us.
Lord, help us to trust you more
and to put our lives in your hands!
O God of unceasing love,
to you be honour, glory and praise. Amen.

Belize

6

May the life of the true vine, enfold us,
may the vigour of the true vine, enliven us, and
may the abundance of the true vine
mark our every effort, for Jesus' sake.

UK

7

Give us strength to understand and eyes to see,
teach us to walk the soft earth
as relatives to all that lives.

Native American

8

Refrain
Glory to Thee, O God of Life
Glory to Thee, O God of Life
Glory to Thee, O God.
Glory to Thee, O God of Life
Glory to Thee, O God.

From the guiding lamp of the ocean
Be hand on the water's helm.
Be love behind the willows,
Be the wind within my sails.

Refrain

Be my prayer, O God,
In accord with thy sanctifying.
Be my heart, O God,
In accord with thy loving care.

Refrain

Be my deed on the land,
In accord with thy satisfying.
Be my wish on the sea,
In accord with thy Holy Plan.

Refrain

USA

9

As the air sings with songs of glory,
as the water flashes with the silver of creation,
as the forest blooms with leaves for the healing of nations,
so may God's light and love
fill our hearts and souls and minds.

UK

10

Lord, let my prayers not cease
when I leave the house of God.
My thoughts in daily life, and my actions in my home
must reflect the joy I feel in the sanctuary.
May each moment I spend in the sanctuary
remain an abiding inspiration in my daily life.
Amen.

UK/Jewish

11

O God, our creator,
by whose mercies and might the world turns safely into darkness
   and returns again to light:
we give into your hands our unfinished tasks, our unsolved
   problems, our unfulfilled hopes,
knowing that only those things which you bless will prosper.
To your great love and protection we commit each other and all
   for whom we pray,
knowing that you alone are our sure defender,
through Jesus Christ our Lord.
Amen.

The Pacific

12

Jesus Christ,
May your love be as embracing
as the oceans around Australia's shores;
your grace as permanent as Uluru (Ayers Rock);
and may your spirit search us out
wherever we may be, and having found us,
never let us go.
Go! For your God goes with you.

Australia

13

BLESSING FOR A PERSON LIVING WITH AIDS

Compassionate God,
look with love on (*names*), whom we love and cherish.
Our hearts are filled with sorrow because they are living with
   AIDS.
We grieve with them all the losses this has already brought,
and are concerned about those that lie ahead.
Therefore, we ask your blessing on them today.

Give (*names*) an even stronger sense of your care for them,
that it might sustain and comfort them always.
Help them to know that you love them with an everlasting love
that is faithful and tender.

Still the terror of their hearts when fear arises and begins to take
hold within.
Let them hear the words of reassurance that you have spoken to
your friends throughout time:
'Fear not, I will be with you.'

Open their spirit to the beauty and gifts of each day.
Help them to live every moment, fully taking in all that it has to
offer which is life-giving, nourishing, inspiring.

Free them from any burdens of guilt and anxiety;
speak your words of forgiveness and lift off all that clouds their
sense that you are there for them.

Heal them in all the ways that are in keeping with your purpose.
We wish long life for them, and freedom from pain and suffering.
May they experience the healing embrace of your Son,
who restored people to themselves.

We ask your blessing, too, on all of us who love them.
May we know how to support them well and be the sacrament of
your care for them.
Enliven us when we lose hope, and strengthen us when we are
weary.
Touch the hearts of those they love who have not been with them.
Bring them to their side.

We thank you for all the ways in which you have shown us your
care,
and for the blessings we have experienced through (*names*) as they
have allowed us to make this journey with them.
We are grateful for all that they give us.

We pray this in your Son, who has told us that he is the
resurrection and the life, and in your Spirit who creates
and heals. Amen.

South Africa

Appendix

HIV/AIDS QUIZ

Ask members of the congregation to write the answers to the following questions.

1 At the end of 2000, how many adults were living with AIDS world-wide?
   a) 5 million   b) 15 million   c) 35 million   d) 50 million
2 In Zambia, what percentage of children has lost one or more parents to AIDS?
   a) 10 per cent   b) 25 per cent   c) 35 per cent
3 I can become infected with HIV by swimming in a pool, sitting in a bath or holding or kissing someone with HIV/AIDS. True or False?
4 HIV/AIDS is incurable. True or False?
5 If a woman is HIV-positive and pregnant, there are medicines that can greatly decrease the chances of her baby becoming infected with HIV. True or False?
6 If I were infected with HIV, I would know because I would feel sick. True or False?
7 HIV/AIDS new combination drug therapies have slowed the progress from HIV through to AIDS in developed countries so that infected people are living longer. True or False?
8 It is safe to extend friendship and support to people living with HIV and AIDS. True or False?

Answers

1 c	5 True
2 b	6 False
3 False	7 True
4 True	8 True

Source: UNAIDS and World Health Organization

Sources and Acknowledgements

Special thanks must be extended to Karin Jonsson, without whose early work and tireless help *From Shore to Shore* would not have happened. Grateful thanks also to the Revd Christopher Burkett and Kate Fyfe for their advice, to Jerry Drino, Elizabeth Harris, Clare Amos, Anne McConnell, Maurice Underwood, and to Jonathan Self for his enthusiastic support and copyright tracking skills.

We are grateful to all authors and publishers who have given permission for their material to appear in this book and we apologize to anyone whose copyright we have inadvertently overlooked. USPG would be grateful to know of any omissions for a future edition.

ORDERS OF SERVICE FOR HOLY COMMUNION

A Liturgy to Celebrate Liberation, Barbados
Written by the Revd Dr Michael Clarke for Emancipation Day in Barbados.

A Liturgy from the Independent Church of the Philippines
With thanks to the Iglesia Filipina Independiente (Independent Church of the Philippines).

The Sri Lankan Workers' Mass
The Christian Workers' Fellowship, Sri Lanka. With thanks to Vijaya Vidyasagara and also to Elizabeth Harris, Secretary for Inter-Faith Relations at the Methodist Church, for writing the introduction.

A Celtic Liturgy in the Tradition of the Carmina Gadelica
Adapted from the Celtic tradition by the Revd Jerry Drino. With thanks also to Catherine Campbell and the Diocese of Northern California.

OTHER ORDERS OF SERVICE

Together We Are Strong: An Australian liturgy for International Women's Day
Colleen Geyer, The Uniting Church in Australia, 2001 Gospel and Gender, National Assembly.

A Caribbean Morning Order of Worship, Jamaica
Written by the Revd Dr George Mulrain, Senior Methodist tutor at the United Theological College of the West Indies, formerly Director of

Mission Studies, Vice-Principal and Methodist tutor at the United College of the Ascension, Birmingham, UK. 'Vengan vengan todos' by Lois Kroehler appears in *Caribbean Praise* (2000) compiled by the Revd Dr George Mulrain (a Global Praise Publication of GBGMusik, the General Board of Global Ministries, The United Methodist Church, 475 Riverside Drive, New York, NY 10115).

A South African Service for World AIDS day
Adapted by Kate Fyfe and Kate Wyles, USPG, from a liturgy written by the Revd Canon D. Mills, Diocese of the Highveld, with permission from the Diocese of Johannesburg, Church of the Province of South Africa. Poem by the Revd John Tyler, taken from *In the Shade of His Hand*.

For the Healing of the Nations: An order of service to celebrate creation
Compiled by Kate Wyles, USPG. Opening prayers with symbols from the Uniting Church in Australia, National Social Justice Sunday, *Standing Together in Hope*, 2000. Confession by the Revd Akuila Yabaki, CCF (Citizens Constitutional Forum), Fiji, former Secretary for Asia and the Pacific, Methodist World Church Office, taken from *Living Prayers for Today*, compiled by Maureen Edwards, International Bible Reading Association, 1996, with permission of Christian Education Publications. Offertory prayer by the Revd Canon Fergus King, USPG. Responses to intercessions adapted from Native American prayer, copyright USPG. The Environmental Lord's Prayer, reading and closing prayer are used with kind permission of Eco-Congregation, a programme for churches administered by ENCAMS. Details of the programme are available by calling 01942 612621 or may be seen at *www.encams.org/ecocongregation*

A South Indian Order of Evening Prayer
Taken from *Worship Resources*, the worship resources book published by the Synod of the Church of South India (11–15 January 2002, session XXVIII), by the Revd Paul Francis and the Revd Eileen Thompson. With thanks to the Revd Julie Lipp Nathaniel, USPG.

Chinese Meditations for Christmas and Easter
Compiled by Karin Jonsson. Reflections are taken from *Lilies of the Field* by Wang Weifan, translated and edited by Janice and Philip Wickeri, Foundation for Theological Education in South East Asia, Hong Kong, 1988. 'Ambassadors of the Heavenly Kingdom' by the North-West Spiritual Workers' Fellowship, 'We reverently worship' by Dr F. Y. Zia, an extract from 'Living Water' by Zhang Jiakun, 'Bitter Cup' by Simon Zhao and 'If I am to suffer' all taken from *Prayers and Thoughts of Chinese Christians* by Kim-Kwong Chan and Alan Hunter, Mowbray, 1991. 'Help each one of us' and 'God, creator of heaven' taken from *With All God's People – an ecumenical prayer circle*, WCC Publications. With thanks to the Amity Foundation, China and Caroline Fielder, China desk, CTBI.

PRAYERS AND LITANIES

Gathering/Opening Prayers

1 Lesbian and Gay Christian Movement. With thanks to the Revd Richard Kirker.
2 Geoff Lowson/USPG.
3 Joanildo Buirty. Taken from *More Living Prayers for Today*, compiled by Maureen Edwards, International Bible Reading Association, 1997, with permission of Christian Education Publications.
4 Taken from *Out of the Shadows*, Christian Aid/Dalit Christmas resource, 2001.
5 Jane Ella P. Montenegro. Taken from *Words for Today 1996*, edited by Maureen Edwards, International Bible Reading Association, 1995, with permission of Christian Education Publications.
6 Magali do Nascimento Cunha. Taken from *Words for Today 1996*, edited by Maureen Edwards, International Bible Reading Association, 1995, with permission of Christian Education Publications.
7 Methodist Church in Guatemala, the World Church Office, Methodist Church, London. Taken from *Living Prayers for Today* compiled by Maureen Edwards, International Bible Reading Association, 1996, with permission of Christian Education Publications.
8 Chris Luxton, General Secretary, Papua New Guinea (PNG) Church Partnership.
9 World Federation of Methodist Women, 2001. With thanks to Rosemary Wells, Area President, World Federation of Methodist and Uniting Church Women.

Thanksgiving

1 *New Zealand Prayer Book/He Karakia Mihinare o Aotearoa*. With thanks to the General Synod Office, Province of Aotearoa, New Zealand and Polynesia.
2 Prayer of Thanksgiving from the 'Agpeya'. Published by the Orthodox Centre for Religious Studies and St John the Beloved Publishing House, 168 El Nozha-El Gedida, Heliopolis, Cairo.
3 National Social Responsibility and Justice, Uniting Church of Australia. Taken from *Mission Prayer Handbook*, 2001. With thanks to the Revd Helen Richmond.
4 Stella Bristow, the Leprosy Mission, England and Wales; former Vice-President of the Methodist Conference, 1995–96.

Offertory Prayers

1 Taken from *Out of the Shadows*, Christian Aid/Dalit Christmas resource, 2001.
2 Methodist Church and NCEC's *Partners in Learning*. With thanks to Clare Amos.
3 Pietermaritzburg Agency for Christian Social Awareness, South Africa.

4 *Prayers from a Columban House* by Ian Fraser. Columban House, Iona Cottage, Laggan, Invernesshire, PH20 1AH.
5 Victor Premasagar. Taken from *Words for Today 1996*, edited by Maureen Edwards, International Bible Reading Association, 1995, with permission of Christian Education Publications.
6 Uniting Church in Australia. With thanks to the Revd Helen Richmond.
7 From a banner in St George's Cathedral, Jerusalem, copyright unknown. Taken from *Living Prayers for Today*, compiled by Maureen Edwards, International Bible Reading Association, 1996, with permission of Christian Education Publications.
8 From *Worship in an Indian Context*, edited by Eric J. Lott, United Theological College, Bangalore, South India. With thanks to the Revd Julie Lipp Nathaniel, USPG.
9 Prepared by Sister Immaculate, the Revd Kamala Joel and Ms Malini Devananda. With thanks to Elizabeth Harris, Secretary for Inter-Faith Relations at the Methodist Church.
10 Alan Paton, Anglican Peace and Justice. With thanks to the Revd Canon Christopher Burkett.

Affirmations of Faith
1 Prepared by children for the World Council of Churches (WCC) 7th Assembly, Canberra, 1991. WCC Publications, PO Box 2100, CH-1211 Geneva 2, Switzerland. Taken from *Living Prayers for Today*, compiled by Maureen Edwards, International Bible Reading Association, 1996, with permission of Christian Education Publications.
2 Ayacucho youth group, Peru. Copyright Peru Comision Episcopal de Acion Social, Lima. Taken from *Living Prayers for Today*, compiled by Maureen Edwards, International Bible Reading Association, 1996, with permission of Christian Education Publications.
3 Uniting Church in Australia. With thanks to the Revd Helen Richmond.

Confession and Absolution
1 Adapted by Walter Russell Bowie and taken from from *The Winds of God's Mercy: Litanies for Enlarging our Worship* by Bishop Jeffrey Rowthorn. With thanks to the Revd Jerry Drino.
2 Taken from *Hasten the Time* by the Revd Canon Christopher Burkett, USPG, 2001.
3 Diocese of Northern California's anti-racism curriculum. With thanks to the Revd Jerry Drino.
4 Diocese of Northern California's anti-racism curriculum. With thanks to the Revd Jerry Drino.
5 With thanks to the Revd Dr George Mulrain, as above. Originally appeared in USPG's quarterly magazine, *Transmission*.
6 Diocese of Northern California's anti-racism curriculum. With thanks to the Revd Jerry Drino.

7 Clare Amos, USPG.

8 The Revd Dr Inderjit Bhogal, Director, The Urban Theology Unit, Sheffield and President of Methodist Conference 2000–2001. With thanks to the World Church Office, the Methodist Church.

9 Taken from *Living Prayers for Today*, compiled by Maureen Edwards, International Bible Reading Association, 1996, with permission of Christian Education Publications.

10 The Revd John Pritchard, former General Secretary of the Methodist Church Overseas Division and Chair, Friends of the Church in China.

11 New World Liturgy. Thanks to the Revd Yohan Devananda, director of Devasasana and Elizabeth Harris, Secretary for Inter-Faith Relations at the Methodist Church.

12 The Revd Dr Israel Selvanayagam, Principal of UCA, Birmingham.

Intercessions

1 Taken from *The Cross is Lifted* (SPCK/CLS India – Chandran Devanesen, CSI).

2 Clare Amos, USPG.

3 The Revd Julie Lipp Nathaniel, USPG.

4 Palestinian Christian prayer, originally taken from the Women's World Day of Prayer.

5 The Revd John Pritchard, former General Secretary of the Methodist Church Overseas Division and Chair, Friends of the Church in China.

6 Anon. With thanks to Clare Amos.

7 Methodist Church and NCEC's *Partners in Learning*. With thanks to Clare Amos.

8 Clare Amos/Methodist Church and NCEC's *Partners in Learning*.

9 Clare Amos.

10 The Revd Dr Israel Selvanayagam, Principal of UCA, Birmingham. Taken from *Words for Today 1999*, edited by Maureen Edwards, International Bible Reading Association, 1998, with permission of Christian Education Publications.

11 Adapted by Brian Blancharde from *Intercessions for the Work of the Church Throughout the World*, USPG, 1998.

12 Taken from *Words for Today 1996*, edited by Maureen Edwards, International Bible Reading Association, 1995, with permission of Christian Education Publications.

13 W. Anthony Reynolds, Friends of the Church in China newsletter. Taken from *Every Time and Place: Methodist Prayer Handbook 1995–96*.

14 The Revd Akuila Yabaki, CCF (Citizens Constitutional Forum), Fiji, former Secretary for Asia and the Pacific, Methodist World Church Office. Taken from *Every Time and Place: Methodist Prayer Handbook 1995–96*.

15 Part of a prayer written by Bernard Narakobi, PNG politician. With thanks to Chris Luxton, General Secretary PNG Church Partnership.

16 The Revd Dr Leslie Griffiths, President of the Methodist Conference 1994–95 and former missionary with the Methodist Church in Haiti.
17 The Revd Canon Christopher Burkett/USPG.
18 The Revd Dr Israel Selvanayagam, Principal of UCA, Birmingham.
19 Diocese of the Highveld, South Africa.
20 Diocese of the Highveld, South Africa.
21 The Revd Canon Christopher Burkett.

Adoration and Praise
1 Traditional Zulu.
2 With thanks to Bishop Miguel Tamayo Zaldivar, Uruguay.
3 The Revd Rexina Johnson, Sierra Leone.
4 Ernesto Cardenal, poet, priest and former member of Sandinista government.
5 Prayers for times when we address issues of diversity, injustice and racism. Diocese of Northern California's anti-racism curriculum. With thanks to Revd Jerry Drino.
6 Clare Amos. Originally appeared in the *Methodist Companion to the Lectionary, Year B*, edited by Don Pickard and Judy Jarvis, MPH, 1999.
7 The Revd John Pritchard, former General Secretary of the Methodist Church Overseas Division and Chair, Friends of the Church in China.

Benedictions/Closing Prayers
1 Taken from *Out of the Shadows*, Christian Aid/Dalit Christmas resource, 2001.
2 Linda Rock.
3 Taken from *More Living Prayers for Today*, compiled by Maureen Edwards, International Bible Reading Association, 1996, with permission of Christian Education Publications.
4 Geoff Lowson/USPG.
5 The Revd Lesley G. Anderson, Methodist Church of Belize. Taken from the *Methodist Prayer Handbook*.
6 The Revd Canon Christopher Burkett/USPG.
7 Native American. Taken from the *Methodist Prayer Handbook*.
8 Little Potion Hermitage. With thanks to Revd Jerry Drino.
9 Eco-Congregation (see details above under For the Healing of the Nations), the Churches' Environmental Programme (CTBI).
10 Rabbi Albert Friedlander. Taken from *Words for Today 1996*, edited by Maureen Edwards, International Bible Reading Association, 1995, with permission of Christian Education Publications.
11 PNG Church Partnership. With thanks to Chris Luxton, General Secretary PNG Church Partnership.
12 The Revd Helen Richmond, Uniting Church in Australia.
13 Diocese of the Highveld, South Africa.

Index